Handshakes to Hashtags

A SALES ODESSEY

ANOOP MURALI

Clever Fox® Publishing

Chennai • Bangalore

CLEVER FOX PUBLISHING
Chennai, India

Published by CLEVER FOX PUBLISHING 2025

ISBN: 978-93-6707-602-6

CONTENTS

ACKNOWLEDGMENTS

In the quiet moments of reflection that precede these words, I find myself overwhelmed with gratitude for the multitude of souls who have woven themselves into the tapestry of my life. To each of you, my deepest thanks.

To my cherished parents, C. Saraswathyamma and M. C. Muralidharan Nair: Your love knows no bounds, and your unwavering support has been the cornerstone of my existence. From the moment you brought me into this world, you bestowed upon me the greatest gift of all—your boundless love and belief in my potential.

My beloved wife, Rashmi Rekha Patel: Your presence has been my guiding light through every twist and turn of this journey. In your eyes, I find both solace and challenge, for it is your honest critiques and fiery debates that have sculpted the contours of my life, making it richer and more profound.

To my dear co-brother, Manish Narayan: Your steadfast loyalty has been a beacon of hope during my darkest hours. Your faith in me, even amidst my own shortcomings, is a testament to the depth of your character and the strength of our bond.

Dr. Reena Patel, my sister-in-law and guide: Your wisdom knows no bounds, and your gentle guidance has been a balm to my soul. Your insights and NLP sessions have not only helped me overcome personal obstacles but have also breathed life into these pages, infusing them with depth and clarity.

Jugal Kishore Patel, my brother-in-law and confidant: Your unwavering encouragement has been a source of endless inspiration. Your wisdom and perspective have opened my eyes to new possibilities, enriching both my life and the pages of this book.

To my esteemed colleagues and mentors (both past and present): I am forever indebted for your invaluable teachings and unwavering support. Your wisdom has been a guiding light, illuminating the path forward and infusing this work with depth and insight.

And to my dear friends, whose laughter and camaraderie have been the lifeblood of my existence: I offer my deepest gratitude. Your unwavering support and enduring friendship have been a source of strength and joy, fueling my passion and sustaining me through every trial and triumph.

To each of you—I offer my eternal thanks. This book stands as a testament to the love, support, and wisdom you have bestowed upon me, and I am forever grateful for the privilege of sharing this journey with you.

AUTHOR'S NOTE

As an executive immersed in the dynamics of IT and Mobile Communication industries for over two decades, I've had the privilege of traversing a multifaceted journey marked by innovation, strategic foresight, and relentless pursuit of excellence. In this book, *Handshakes to Hashtags: A Sales Odyssey*, I aim to distill the essence of my experiences, offering actionable insights and proven methodologies for driving long-term growth and cultivating unparalleled success in the ever-evolving business landscape.

Drawing upon my tenure as a top-performing executive, I delve into the intricacies of crafting robust sales strategies, forging strategic partnerships, and executing global business development with precision. From penetrating challenging markets to fostering high-profit accounts and establishing critical relationships with corporate decision-makers, each chapter encapsulates invaluable lessons garnered through years of hands-on experience.

Throughout these pages, I illuminate the transformative power of strong sales techniques and the optimization of sales processes to achieve exceptional results. Using real-world case studies and personal anecdotes, I aim to empower aspiring executives and seasoned leaders alike with the strategic acumen and innovative thinking necessary to thrive in today's competitive landscape.

Whether you're a budding entrepreneur, a seasoned executive, or a business enthusiast eager to unlock the secrets of success, *Handshakes to Hashtags: A Sales Odyssey* offers a roadmap for achieving unparalleled excellence in the fast-paced world of technology and beyond. Embark on this journey with an open mind and a steadfast determination to redefine what's possible in the realm of business leadership.

Together, let's create the path to success and leave an indelible mark on the industries we serve.

Warm regards,

Anoop

INTRODUCTION

In the illustrious corridors of sales academia, where the aroma of freshly brewed coffee mingles with the scent of ambition, I embark on a literary voyage unlike any other. Among the myriad tomes adorning these venerable shelves, my humble contribution emerges—a synthesis of memoir and academia, sprinkled with a pinch of mischief and a dash of whimsy.

In the annals of salesmanship, where the battleground is as diverse as the products vying for attention, I try to create a narrative that traverses epochs of commerce evolution. With the wit of a seasoned storyteller and the wisdom of a sales sage, I embark on a journey from the analog days of door-to-door canvassing to the digital dawn of virtual marketplaces. Join me as I delve into the chronicles of a salesperson extraordinaire.

Spanning decades and continents, this memoir illuminates the path of a frontline sales luminary who began as a foot soldier in the trenches of direct selling, only to ascend to the heights of strategic leadership of technology sales.

As I step into the realm of sales lore, I do not profess to be a flawless paragon but rather a humble protagonist, stumbling through the labyrinthine pathways of commerce with the finesse of a bull in a china shop. My narrative commences in the sepia-toned era of yore, where cold calls held sway and fax machines reigned supreme. From those nostalgic days of door-to-door endeavors, I journeyed through the sands of time, riding the wave of technological advancement into the vibrant world of online commerce.

Through a series of candid reflections and astute observations, I have tried to share invaluable insights gleaned from the front lines of sales warfare. From the challenges of establishing credibility for obscure products to the complexities of navigating ever-shifting market landscapes, each chapter unveils a tapestry of trials and triumphs. Amidst the cacophony of self-proclaimed gurus and sales sages, I offer not a universal remedy but rather an authentic account of my own exploits and escapades. Yes, dear reader, I am well acquainted with the plethora of sales manuals promising untold riches and effortless success. Yet, in the pursuit of scholarly inquiry (and perhaps a tinge of masochistic curiosity), I venture where others fear to tread, delving into the murky depths of my own triumphs and tribulations.

Within these pages lie not just the tried-and-tested techniques of salesmanship but also the unadorned truths of a frontline combatant in the struggle for market dominance. As I recount the highs and lows of my sales odyssey, from the shadows of obscurity to the zenith of corporate leadership, I extend an invitation for you to join me on a voyage of self-discovery and sales enlightenment.

Amidst the cacophony of self-proclaimed gurus and sales sages, I offer not a universal remedy but rather an authentic account of my own exploits and escapades. Within these pages lie not just the tried-and-tested techniques of salesmanship but also the unadorned truths of a frontline combatant in the struggle for market dominance.

At the heart of this narrative lies a pivotal moment of reinvention as I return to the role of a lone crusader in the uncharted territory of working for a startup venture. Through a combination of grit, guile, and genuine human connection, I not only secure the elusive first sale but also catalyze a paradigm shift in organizational vision, propelling a fledgling product into the mainstream spotlight.

With wit and candor, *Handshakes to Hashtags: A Sales Odyssey* offers a roadmap for aspiring sales leaders. Whether you're a seasoned veteran seeking inspiration or a novice embarking on your own sales odyssey, this memoir will serve as a beacon of guidance, illuminating the path to success in the ever-changing landscape of technology sales.

1

FOOTPRINTS IN THE DUST

As I reflect on my career, I can't help but marvel at the incredible transformation that has taken place in the world of sales since the mid-90s. Back then, I was just starting out, armed with nothing but a telephone directory and heaps of determination. Cold calling was the name of the game, and every rejection felt like a personal defeat.

Embarking on a reflective journey through the evolution of salesmanship unveils a profound transformation that has unfolded since the mid-90s. The advent of the internet challenged traditional sales approaches and demanded adaptation to a digital era.

But it was social media that truly revolutionized the game. Platforms like Twitter and Instagram gave me a direct line to consumers, allowing me to engage with them on a personal level. Suddenly, it wasn't just about selling a product; it was about building relationships, fostering loyalty, and earning trust. Of course, with all this digital interaction came an avalanche of data. Every click, every like, every share provided valuable insights into consumer behavior. I had to become adept at mining this data, extracting nuggets of wisdom that would guide my approach and help me stay ahead of the curve.

But perhaps the most profound change of all was the empowerment of the consumer. No longer content to be passive spectators in the sales process, they demanded to be heard, to be valued. And I had to listen, to adapt, to meet their needs in ways I never thought possible. With all the twists and turns of this change, one thing remains constant: the need to embrace change, to innovate, to navigate the ever-shifting landscape of the digital frontier. From handshakes to hashtags, it's been quite the journey. And I can't wait to see where it takes me next.

In the hazy glow of memory, time slows and nostalgia reigns supreme—a place where the echoes of footsteps on cobblestone streets linger long after the last passerby has disappeared into the folds of history. It is within this ethereal landscape that my journey begins, amidst the sepia-toned vignettes of a bygone era.

Long before the advent of hashtags and digital handshakes, there existed a simpler time—a time when salesmanship was an art practiced with the finesse of a seasoned performer, and success was measured not in clicks and conversions, but in the firmness of a handshake and the sincerity of a smile. In the early days, a salesperson's appearance held significant importance, with companies providing training not only on etiquette, communication, and body language but also on dressing appropriately, even down to the correct way of shaking hands.

In those days of analog allure, I embarked on my maiden voyage into the realm of gadgets and technology—a place ripe with promise yet fraught with uncertainty. Picture this: I was peddling desktop computers with configurations so modest that today's tech-savvy folks would scoff, dubbing them relics of fiction. Ah, the nostalgia! It was the era of the 586 series, and I had the privilege of witnessing the grand launch of Intel's inaugural Pentium processors.

Imagine me, adorned in my reliable motorcycle gear, a bag brimming with brochures, specification sheets, and order forms slung securely over my shoulder, as I maneuvered through the lively industrial quarters of Bangalore, the bustling heart of India's IT landscape. With no scheduled appointments to rely on, I embarked on a daring mission of door-to-door visits to prospective clients. Ah, those were the days before emails became the go-to communication tool! Each call I made was a roll of the dice, every encounter with a receptionist presenting an opportunity to establish a meaningful connection. Nurturing a bond with these gatekeepers was paramount, for they wielded the power to grant access to the enigmatic decision-makers hidden behind closed doors.

And oh, the sheer determination required! Every knock on a door was a step closer to filling our sales funnel, a testament to the relentless pursuit of prospects. Armed with nothing but dreams and a fervent desire to etch my name in the annals of sales history, I embarked on a journey that would define my destiny. But let's not forget the importance of appearances! Back then, a salesperson's attire spoke volumes. Companies even provided tips on dressing etiquette alongside soft skills training—because, after all, a firm handshake and a polished demeanor could make or break a deal.

Ah, reminiscing about the past brings forth a flood of memories! I recall the countless hours I dedicated to traversing neighborhoods, pounding the pavement, and diligently knocking on doors.

Each dusty sidewalk served as a testament to my unwavering determination and relentless pursuit of mastering the art of salesmanship. Amidst rejection and disillusionment lurked moments of triumph—small victories that illuminated the path ahead. From the exhilaration of closing that inaugural deal to the satisfaction of earning the trust and respect of loyal clients, each milestone fueled my passion and propelled me forward.

As we embark on the journey to becoming exceptional salespeople, it's crucial to acknowledge the indispensable qualities of persistence and perseverance. These virtues, along with several others that we'll delve into in the upcoming chapters, form the bedrock of success in the world of sales.

Be prepared to experience not just the tales of a sales luminary, but the timeless truths of a profession steeped in human connection and fueled by the pursuit of excellence. Furthermore, we must recognize that rejections and disillusionment are inevitable challenges that salespeople face regularly. In this book, we will not only discuss techniques for handling these situations but also how to transform them into opportunities for personal and professional growth.

From the exhilaration of closing my first sale to the gratification of earning the trust and respect of loyal customers, each achievement fueled my passion and propelled me forward. Within these pages lie not just stories of a salesperson extraordinaire, but timeless truths of a profession rooted in human connection and driven by the pursuit of excellence.

Sales has evolved significantly—from the arduous days of door-to-door canvassing to the comfort of one's office or home. With all the changes through the ages, one fundamental aspect remains paramount—communication. So, let me begin at the beginning—understanding the significance of mastering sales techniques and efficiently managing the sales cycle in today's age and time.

I'm no sales guru, but just a regular Joe sharing tales from the sales trenches. And what have I to offer here? I've concocted a potion of wisdom brewed from the bubbling cauldron of my experiences. It's like having a recipe for success, but instead of baking cookies, we're cooking up killer sales strategies! Stick with me, and together we'll unlock the secrets to becoming a sales superstar. Think of it as our own little adventure, with me as your trusty guide through the wilds of commerce. So, grab your metaphorical compass and let's chart a course to sales greatness. Who knows, maybe one day we'll look back and laugh at the absurdity of it all while sipping champagne from the pinnacle of sales success! As the great Zig Ziglar once said, "You don't have to be great to start, but you have to start to be great."

But wait! Before we dive headfirst into the depths of effective communication, let's indulge in some academic humor and humorous anecdotes. After all, what's a sales journey without a sprinkling of wit and charm?

Allow me to regale you with a humorous anecdote from my early days in sales!

Picture this: A bright-eyed, bushy-tailed salesperson, armed with nothing but a pocketful of dreams and a knack for persuasion, sets out on his daily rounds on a rusty motorcycle. Now, imagine me, braving the sweltering heat of Bangalore's industrial districts, weaving through the infamous heavy traffic like a seasoned pro.

One fateful day, as I made my rounds, I stumbled upon a particularly imposing office building. Determined to make my mark, I marched up to the entrance with a huge dose of confidence. But alas, fate had other plans.

As I confidently strode through the door, I found myself face-to-face with the most formidable foe of all: the receptionist. With a glance that could freeze molten lava, she sized me up from head to toe, clearly unimpressed by my sales spiel.

Undeterred, I extended my hand for a handshake, only to realize too late that my palms were clammy with nervous sweat. With a sheepish grin, I attempted to recover, offering a joke about the weather that fell flatter than yesterday's soda.

But here's where the real comedy begins. Just as I was about to make my grand exit, my trusty motorcycle, parked outside, decided to join the fun. With a deafening roar, it let out a puff of smoke that enveloped the entire lobby, leaving me standing there like a deer caught in headlights.

Needless to say, my chances of sealing the deal evaporated faster than ice cream on a hot summer's day. But hey, every failure is just another opportunity for a good laugh, right?

And so, dear reader, as we embark on this journey of self-discovery and sales enlightenment, let us not forget to embrace the mishaps and blunders along the way. After all, what's life without a little humor to spice things up?

2

FOUNDATIONS OF SALES EXCELLENCE—KEY QUALITIES FOR SUCCESS

Great salespeople possess a mix of inherent traits and learned skills. Here are some of the most fundamental qualities:

1. Communication Skills
2. Empathy
3. Confidence
4. Resilience
5. Product Knowledge
6. Problem-Solving Skills
7. Persistence
8. Adaptability
9. Integrity
10. Goal Orientation

1. Communication Skills

Being able to articulate ideas clearly and persuasively is essential in sales. This includes active listening, asking probing questions, and adapting communication style to different clients.

Active Listening

Think of active listening as the superhero cape of communication skills. It's not just about hearing words; it's about understanding the underlying emotions and intentions. Imagine you're selling insurance, and your client starts talking about their fear of unexpected medical bills. Instead of immediately launching into your pitch about the benefits of your coverage, take a moment to empathize and acknowledge their concerns. Say something like, "I hear you. Medical expenses can be a real headache, figuratively and literally!"

Active listening is a fundamental communication skill that goes beyond simply hearing what someone is saying. It involves fully engaging with the speaker, listening not only to what is being said but also to what is left unsaid or partially said. Let's break down the scenario of selling insurance and how active listening plays a crucial role:

- **Listen attentively**: When your client expresses their fear of unexpected medical bills, it's essential to pay close attention to both their words and their non-verbal cues. This means maintaining eye contact, nodding occasionally to show you're following along, and being genuinely present in the conversation.
- **Understand the emotions:** Try to understand the underlying emotions behind what the client is saying. In this case, it's fear and concern about potential financial burdens due to medical expenses. Acknowledging these emotions shows that you're tuned into their perspective and are empathetic to their situation.
- **Reflect and empathize:** Instead of immediately jumping into your sales pitch, take a moment to reflect on what you've heard and empathize with the client's concerns. You might say something like, "I understand how worrying it can be to think

about unexpected medical bills. It's something that many people find stressful."

- **Validate their feelings:** Let the client know that their concerns are valid and understandable. This validation helps build rapport and trust because it shows that you're not dismissing their worries but rather acknowledging them as legitimate.
- **Connect to your product/service:** Once you've established a connection and validated the client's feelings, you can then naturally transition to discussing how your insurance coverage can help alleviate their concerns. For example, you might say, "Given your concerns about medical expenses, our insurance plan offers comprehensive coverage that can provide peace of mind in these situations."

By actively listening and empathizing with your client's concerns before diving into your sales pitch, you demonstrate genuine care and understanding. This approach not only builds rapport but also increases the likelihood of your client being receptive to your message and more inclined to consider your product or service.

I remember a particularly memorable encounter while selling desktop computers to an end user. As I began discussing the benefits of our latest models, the customer suddenly veered off topic, expressing their anxiety about the rapid pace of technological advancements. They launched into a comical tirade about their fear of being left behind in the digital age, envisioning a dystopian future where their outdated computer would become an artifact in a museum of ancient technology. Despite my initial surprise, I found myself chuckling along with them, recognizing the humor in their exaggerated fears.

After a moment of shared laughter, I acknowledged their concerns, jokingly assuring them that their new computer wouldn't become an exhibit anytime soon. This light-hearted exchange helped ease the tension and opened the door for a more relaxed conversation about their specific computing needs. In the end, we were able to find the perfect desktop solution that not only met their technical requirements but also provided reassurance that they wouldn't be left behind in the ever-evolving world of technology. It was a reminder that even in the midst of a sales pitch, a touch of humor and empathy can go a long way in building rapport with customers.

Asking Probing Questions

Sales is a bit like detective work. You need to uncover your client's needs and pain points before you can offer a solution. Asking open-ended questions helps you gather valuable information and build rapport. For instance, if you're selling software, you might ask, "What challenges are you currently facing with your current system?" Remember, the goal is to dig deeper without making your client feel like they're under interrogation. A little finesse goes a long way!

Picture yourself as the Sherlock Holmes of sales, armed not with a magnifying glass but with a finely crafted set of open-ended questions. Your mission? To unravel the mysteries of your client's needs and desires without them feeling like they're in the hot seat.

So, let's dive into this detective work, shall we? Imagine you're selling software, and your potential client runs a bustling e-commerce site. You start by mildly probing questions like,

"What are the biggest headaches you face while managing your online store?" This question isn't just about uncovering problems; it's about creating a comfortable space for your client to share their pain points. Now, here's where the finesse comes in. You don't want your interrogation—I mean, conversation—to feel like an intense grilling session. Instead, sprinkle in some subtle wit and humor to keep things light. Maybe throw in a quip like, "I bet dealing with those website glitches feels like fighting a never-ending battle with gremlins in the server room!"

As your client chuckles at your clever analogy, they'll start opening up more. They might respond with, "Oh, you have no idea! It's like our website has a mind of its own sometimes." Bingo! You've struck gold. Now you can delve deeper, asking follow-up questions like, "How do these glitches impact your sales and customer satisfaction?"

By blending your detective skills with a touch of humor, you're not only gathering valuable intel but also building rapport. Your client sees you as more than just a salesperson; you're a trusted advisor who understands their pain points and isn't afraid to crack a joke or two along the way.

Remember, the key is to keep the conversation flowing naturally and make your client feel heard and understood. So, channel your inner Sherlock, sprinkle in some charm, and watch as your sales game reaches new heights!

Adapting Communication Style

One size rarely fits all in sales. Your communication style should be as flexible as a yoga instructor doing the downward dog. Tailor your approach to each client based on their personality, preferences, and communication style. If you're dealing with a no-nonsense CEO, cut straight to the facts. If you're wooing a more laid-back client, sprinkle in some humor and charm. Just be careful not to overdo it; you don't want your sales pitch to sound like a stand-up routine!

Let's delve into the idea of adapting communication styles in sales with some examples:

Example 1: No-Nonsense CEO

Imagine you're pitching a product to a CEO known for being direct and results oriented. In this scenario, it's best to cut straight to the chase. Provide clear and concise information about how your product or service can solve their specific pain points. Stick to the facts, emphasize ROI, and avoid fluff or unnecessary details. For instance, you might say something like:

"Mr. Johnson, I understand you're focused on increasing efficiency in your operations. Our software has been proven to reduce processing time by 30%, leading to significant cost savings for companies like yours."

Example 2: Laid-back Client

On the other hand, if you're dealing with a client who prefers a more laid-back approach, injecting some humor and charm into your communication can be effective. Take the time to build rapport and establish a connection before diving into the sales pitch. You might share a relevant anecdote or use a light-hearted analogy to make your point. For example:

"Hey there, Sarah! Before we dive into the details, did I tell you about the time our product saved a client's day? It's like having a superhero on your team, but without the cape!"

Example 3: Analytical Decision Maker

When dealing with a client who is analytical and detail-oriented, focus on providing comprehensive information and data to support your claims. Take a more structured approach, presenting evidence, case studies, and testimonials to demonstrate the effectiveness of your solution. Avoid vague promises; instead, offer concrete evidence of success. For instance:

"John, I know you like to see the numbers. Our latest study shows a 40% increase in customer satisfaction within the first three months of implementing our services. Let me walk you through the data."

Example 4: Relationship-Oriented Client

For clients who prioritize relationships and trust, take the time to listen actively and show genuine interest in their needs and concerns. Emphasize the long-term value of your partnership and how your product or service can contribute to their success. Share stories of other satisfied clients and highlight the personalized support they can expect. You might say something like:

"Lisa, I appreciate the importance of trust in our partnership. Let me share how we've worked closely with similar companies to tailor solutions that meet their unique challenges. I'm here to support you every step of the way."

Remember, the key is to adapt your communication style based on the individual preferences and personality of each client. By doing so, you can build stronger relationships, increase trust, and ultimately, improve your chances of making a successful sale.

The gist of the matter is smooth talk that can weave its way around people and situations is the key to personal growth. Intrigued? Let's dive in.

Adaptability: You must have been in situations where you changed your course after judging the scenario was completely different from your expectations. Your ability to adapt will bring in more success than learning all the theories of sales management.

Control: Mastering the art of words lets you fine tune any situation, from office politics to Sunday brunch drama. Ever watched a top salesperson in action? It's like watching a magician pull off a flawless trick—effortless, engaging, and completely in control. But here's the secret: It's not just about the pitch; it's about having the right tools and knowing how to use them. Enter resistance bands—the unsung heroes of fitness. Just like a great salesperson can turn a simple conversation into a deal, these bands transform even the smallest space into a full-body workout.

First up, adaptability. A great salesperson doesn't use the same pitch on every client; they adjust to the person in front of them. Resistance bands do the same, flexing to match your strength level and goals. Whether you're closing a deal or building muscle, success is all about knowing when to apply pressure and when to ease up.

Then there's portability. A high-performing salesperson doesn't need a fancy office to make things happen—give them a phone and a solid product, and they'll sell from anywhere. Resistance bands follow the same logic. No gym? No problem. Gains don't wait, just like opportunities in sales. The best communicators and fitness enthusiasts alike know how to make things work, whether they're in a conference room or a hotel room.

Now, let's talk control. A skilled salesperson guides a conversation like a conductor leading an orchestra—confident, intentional, and always aware of the rhythm. Resistance bands demand the same precision, challenging your muscles while keeping every movement smooth and controlled. Sloppy form won't get you results in the gym, just like an aggressive, pushy sales approach won't close deals. It's all about finesse.

And of course, the long game. Sales isn't just about making one deal—it's about building relationships, just like fitness is about consistency. Resistance bands strengthen your body while protecting your joints, much like a well-crafted sales strategy strengthens your career while safeguarding your reputation. But here's the kicker: One tool alone won't make you a top performer. Just as no single sales tactic guarantees success, you need a mix of skills—listening, negotiating, and knowing when to seal the deal. And when all else fails, remember: The best salespeople, like the best communicators, know that success isn't just about what you say—it's about how and when you say it. Read the customer, adjust your approach, and close with confidence. Easy, right?

The Language of Sales: Ever notice how sales jargon can sound like a foreign language? It's like a secret code only salespeople understand. Imagine you're in a meeting, and your client says, "We're looking for a scalable solution with seamless integration." Translation: *Please, save us from this tech nightmare!* Don't worry; you don't need a decoder ring. Just remember to speak the universal language of benefits and solutions, with a dose of empathy and understanding.

In sales, mastering communication isn't just about talking; it's about connecting. So, channel your inner conversationalist, sprinkle in some humor when appropriate, and watch those deals roll in!

2. Empathy

Understanding the needs and concerns of customers is crucial for building trust and rapport. Empathetic salespeople can connect with clients on a deeper level and tailor solutions to their specific situations.

Think of empathy as the secret sauce in the recipe for successful sales. It's not just about pushing products; it's about understanding the person on the other end of the transaction, their needs, desires, and even their quirks. Imagine you walk into a shoe store, and the salesperson greets you with a warm smile and a genuine interest in your footwear needs. They don't just shove the latest sneakers in your face; instead, they ask about your preferences or your lifestyle,. Suddenly, you're not just a customer; you're a person with a story, and they're there to help you walk comfortably through it.

Empathy transforms a transaction into a relationship. Let's say you're selling insurance. Sure, you could bombard your potential client with statistics and scare tactics about the dangers of not being insured. But what if you took a moment to understand their fears, their hopes, and their dreams? Maybe they're worried about leaving their family financially vulnerable if something were to happen to them. By tapping into that emotional connection, you can tailor your pitch to address their specific needs and provide peace of mind. So, next time you're in a sales situation, remember empathy isn't just good for the soul; it's good for business.

And never forgot the power of wit and humor. When used appropriately and wisely, they can not put the customer at ease but make the whole experience memorable.

3. Confidence

Confidence is like the glitter glue that holds a sales pitch together—it adds sparkle and makes everything stick. Let's move on, shall we?

Confidence adds flavor, zest, and trust that makes the customer think, "Hey, these guys know what they're doing!" Think about it this way: Would you buy a parachute from someone who's nervously fidgeting and looking around as if they're about to jump out of a plane for the first time themselves? Probably not. But a salesperson who confidently assures you that their parachutes have been tested by daredevil experts and are guaranteed to make you feel like a flying squirrel? Now, that's someone you'd trust to keep you from becoming a pancake.

Let's break it down further. Picture yourself walking into a car dealership. You're met by two salespeople. One is slouched behind their desk, blank and disinterested, and unsure of what to say. The other is standing tall, smiling, and confidently greeting you like they're about to sell you the ride of your dreams. Who are you more likely to believe when they say that the car you're eyeing is the smoothest ride this side of equator?

Confidence isn't just about puffing out your chest and pretending you know everything. It's about genuinely believing in what you're offering and being able to convey that belief to others.

Imagine you're about to sell ice to an Eskimo. Now, would you do it with sweaty palms and a shaky voice, or would you confidently strut in there like you're selling sunshine in a bottle? Exactly! Confidence is key.

So, in the world of sales, confidence isn't just a nice-to-have; it's the magic ingredient that turns maybes into yeses and skeptical frowns into satisfied smiles. However, it will be prudent to remember, confidence sells, but arrogance smells—nobody wants to buy from a salesperson who thinks they're the gift to humanity wrapped in a shiny sales pitch.

Here's the scoop: Confidence isn't just about talking the talk; it's about walking the walk too. You've got to genuinely believe in what you're selling, whether it's a revolutionary mop or the next big thing in tech. If you're not convinced, why should your customer be?

Now, onto the fun part: building that unshakable confidence. Think of it like going to the gym for your self-esteem. You've got to work those confidence muscles regularly to see results. Here are some easy tips:

- ✓ **Practice Positive Affirmations**: Start your day with a pep talk in the mirror. Tell yourself you're a sales superstar, and soon enough, you'll start believing it too.
- ✓ **Set Achievable Goals**: Break down your sales targets into bite-sized chunks. Achieving small wins regularly will boost your confidence and keep you motivated.
- ✓ **Know Your Stuff**: Become a walking encyclopedia of your product or service. The more you know, the easier it is to talk about it with confidence.
- ✓ **Embrace Failure**: Yes, you heard me right. Every "no" is just one step closer to a "yes". Learn from your mistakes, dust yourself off, and keep pushing forward.
- ✓ **Dress the Part**: You know what they say: dress for success! When you look good, you feel good, and that confidence will shine through your interactions.
- ✓ **Practice Power Poses**: Strike a superhero pose before a big presentation. It might sound silly, but studies show it can actually boost your confidence levels.
- ✓ **Seek Feedback**: Don't be afraid to ask for feedback from colleagues or mentors. Constructive criticism can help you identify areas for improvement and build confidence in your abilities.

Remember, Rome wasn't built in a day, and neither is confidence. It's a journey, not a destination. So, go out there, strut your stuff, and let that confidence shine! You've got this!

4. Resilience

Rejection is inevitable in sales, but top performers don't let it deter them. They bounce back quickly from setbacks, learn from failures, and stay motivated to pursue new opportunities.

Sales, often dubbed as the art of persuasion, is a field rife with rejection. However, top performers possess an unwavering resilience that allows them to weather these setbacks with grace and determination.

Examples of Resilience in Action:

The Persistent Prospector: Imagine a salesperson diligently cold-calling potential clients, only to face rejection after rejection. Instead of being discouraged, they analyze their approach, refine their pitch, and persist until they secure a sale. This resilience turns setbacks into stepping stones toward success.

Turning "No" to "Yes": Picture a sales representative pitching a product to a skeptical customer who initially rejects the offer. Rather than giving up, they use the rejection as an opportunity to address concerns, build rapport, and ultimately convert the rejection into a sale.

Tips for Overcoming Rejection:

1. Reframe Rejection:

Tip: Treat rejection as feedback rather than failure. Embrace it as an opportunity to refine your approach.

2. Learn from Setbacks:

Tip: Analyze each rejection to identify patterns and areas for improvement. Adapt your strategy accordingly to increase your chances of success in future interactions.

3. Maintain Motivation:

Tip: Focus on your long-term goals and the potential rewards of success. Stay motivated by visualizing your achievements and reminding yourself of the value you bring to your clients.

4. Cultivate Resilience:

Tip: Develop resilience by practicing self-care, maintaining a positive mindset, and seeking support from colleagues and mentors. Remember, resilience is like a muscle that strengthens with use.

5. Embrace Failure:

Tip: Shift your perspective on failure from something to be feared to a natural part of the learning process. Each rejection is an opportunity to grow and refine your skills.

In the unpredictable terrain of sales, rejection is not a roadblock, but a springboard to success. By embodying resilience, sales professionals can bounce back from setbacks, learn from failures, and remain steadfast in their pursuit of new opportunities. So, embrace rejection, learn from it, and let it fuel your journey to sales excellence.

"Sales is like a game of dodgeball; you're bound to get hit with rejection, but the best players turn those rejections into epic comeback stories."

5. Product Knowledge

Knowledge of the product or service being sold is vital. Nothing can replace this. Having in-depth knowledge of the product or service you're selling is indeed crucial for effectively addressing customer inquiries, overcoming objections, and demonstrating value. Here's a comprehensive breakdown along with some practical tips and examples:

Understanding the Product Inside Out

- Familiarize yourself with every aspect of the product or service. This includes its features, functionalities, benefits, and unique selling points.

For example, if you're selling a new smartphone, know its technical specifications, camera capabilities, battery life, and any innovative features it offers, such as facial recognition or augmented reality technology.

Stay Updated on Industry Trends

- Keep abreast of the latest developments, innovations, and trends within your industry. This will enable you to anticipate customer questions and position your product or service effectively.
- Follow industry blogs, attend conferences, and subscribe to relevant newsletters to stay informed.

For instance, if you're selling software solutions, stay informed about emerging technologies like artificial intelligence, machine learning, and blockchain, and how they can benefit your customers.

Know Your Competition

- Understand the competitive landscape and how your product or service compares to others in the market.
- Identify your competitors' strengths and weaknesses to effectively differentiate your offering.
- Conduct competitive analysis regularly to stay updated on their latest offerings and strategies.

For example, if you're selling fitness equipment, understand the features and pricing of similar products offered by other brands, and highlight what sets your product apart, such as superior durability or advanced tracking capabilities.

Continuously Educate Yourself

- Invest time in ongoing learning and training to deepen your knowledge and skills.

- Utilize resources such as online courses, webinars, and workshops provided by your company or industry associations.

For instance, if you're selling financial services, stay updated on changes in regulations, investment strategies, and economic trends to provide informed advice to your clients.

Listen to Customer Feedback

- Pay attention to customer feedback and use it to improve your product knowledge and sales approach.
- Actively seek feedback through surveys, reviews, and direct interactions with customers.
- Address any common concerns or misconceptions by updating your knowledge and providing accurate information.

For example, if customers frequently ask about the compatibility of your product with other devices, ensure you have a thorough understanding of its integration capabilities and can provide clear explanations.

By following these tips and continuously honing your product knowledge, you'll be better equipped to handle customer inquiries, address objections, and ultimately drive sales. Remember, a well-informed and knowledgeable salesperson instills confidence in customers, improves the probability of a sale considerably, and enhances the overall buying experience.

6. Problem-Solving Skills

Sales often involve navigating complex situations and overcoming obstacles. Great salespeople are resourceful and can think on their feet to find creative solutions that meet the customer's needs, so let's delve into the fascinating world of sales problem-solving skills with a dash of wit!

1. **The Power of Resourcefulness:**

Salespeople often find themselves in situations akin to navigating a labyrinth, with unexpected twists and turns. The key to success? Embracing your inner MacGyver! Just like the resourceful TV character, great salespeople can fashion solutions from seemingly mundane objects.

2. **Flexibility and Adaptability:**

In the dynamic world of sales, adaptability is key. Think of a skilled chef preparing meals for a diverse group of guests. One diner might crave a spicy, exotic dish, while another prefers a classic, comforting meal. To satisfy both, the chef adjusts ingredients and presentation to match their tastes. Similarly, a salesperson must tailor their approach to fit each client's preferences. A data-driven executive may respond best to detailed analytics, while a relationship-focused entrepreneur might value a warm, conversational approach. By reading the room and adjusting your style, you can turn differences into opportunities for success.

3. **Creative Problem-Solving:**

Ah, the art of turning lemons into lemonade! Great salespeople possess a knack for seeing problems not as roadblocks, but as puzzles waiting to be solved. Picture this: You're facing a tight deadline to close a deal, but your usual approach isn't yielding results. Time to unleash your inner Sherlock Holmes! Get curious, explore alternative strategies, and don't be afraid to think outside the box. Perhaps a personalized video message or a surprise gift could tip the scales in your favor. Remember, creativity is your secret weapon in the battle against sales woes.

Tips for Staying Ahead:

- ✓ **Embrace Lifelong Learning:** Just like wine, knowledge improves with age. Stay abreast of the latest trends, technologies, and techniques in the sales industry through continuous learning. Attend workshops, read industry publications, and network with fellow sales professionals to expand your repertoire of problem-solving strategies.
- ✓ **Foster a Growth Mindset:** In the words of the great philosopher Socrates, "The only true wisdom is in knowing you know nothing." Approach each challenge with an open mind and a willingness to learn from both successes and failures. Cultivate a growth mindset that thrives on experimentation and adaptation and watch your problem-solving prowess soar to new heights.
- ✓ **Build a Support Network:** Behind every successful salesperson is a team of allies ready to offer guidance and support. Surround yourself with mentors, colleagues, and industry experts who can provide valuable insights and fresh perspectives. Don't hesitate to seek advice or collaborate with others when faced with a particularly thorny problem; two heads (or three, or four) are often better than one!

Mastering the art of sales problem-solving is like embarking on a thrilling adventure filled with twists, turns, and the occasional plot twist. By honing your resourcefulness, flexibility, creativity, and staying committed to lifelong learning, you'll be well-equipped to navigate even the most treacherous sales terrain with ease.

7. Persistence

Successful salespeople are persistent without being pushy. They follow up diligently, overcome objections, and remain focused on achieving their goals. Persistence in sales is like the secret sauce that makes the difference between a successful salesperson and a mediocre one.

Picture it like this: You're on a quest, battling objections and navigating through the treacherous waters of customer hesitations. But fear not, brave sales warrior! With the right mindset and strategies, victory shall be yours!

Firstly, let's debunk the myth that persistence equals pushiness. No! Successful salespeople possess a finesse, a delicate balance between tenacity and charm. They don't bulldoze their way through objections; instead, they dance around them like skilled matadors, gracefully dodging each jab with finesse.

Now, how does one cultivate this art of persistent charm? Fear not, for I shall bestow upon you the wisdom of the ages (or at least some solid sales advice).

Establish Rapport: Before diving headfirst into the sales pitch, take a moment to build rapport with your potential client. Ask about their day, share a joke, or bond over a mutual interest.

Remember, people are more likely to listen to someone they feel a connection with.

Example: "Ah, Mr. Johnson, I couldn't help but notice your vast literature collection. I, too, am a voracious reader. Now, let's talk about how our product can revolutionize your reading experience!"

Follow-Up, Follow-Up, Follow-Up: Ah, the cornerstone of persistence! A single follow-up is like a pebble in the pond, but a series of follow-ups creates ripples that eventually lead to the shores of success. Be diligent in your follow-up efforts but remember to strike a balance between being tenacious and becoming a nuisance.

Example: "Dear Mr. Thompson, I hope this message finds you well. I wanted to follow up on our previous conversation and address any lingering questions you may have about our product. Shall we schedule a time to chat further?"

Objection Handling: Ah, the thrill of the verbal joust! When faced with objections, don your metaphorical armor and prepare for battle. But remember, the goal isn't to defeat your opponent but to understand their concerns and address them with finesse.

Example: "I understand your concern about the upfront cost, Ms. Rodriguez. However, let me break down the long-term savings our product offers, making it a wise investment for your business."

My dear salespeople, persistence is not merely a trait but a way of life in the realm of sales. Armed with charm, wit, and a dash of humor, you shall conquer the sales landscape with grace and finesse. Onward, to victory!

8. Adaptability

The sales landscape is constantly evolving, so the ability to adapt to changing market conditions, customer preferences, and new technologies is essential for long-term success. Embracing adaptability in the sales landscape is like being a chameleon at a color palette convention—you need to be able to change hues at a moment's notice! Let's break down this essential trait with practical tips:

Stay Informed, Stay Relevant: Just like keeping up with the Kardashians, staying abreast of market trends, customer behaviors, and emerging technologies is crucial. Whether it's through industry publications, webinars, or networking events, make sure your knowledge is as up to date as the latest meme.

Flexibility Is Key: Remember, rigidity is for office chairs, not sales strategies. Whether it's shifting your approach to suit different customer personas or adapting your pitch to align with current trends, flexibility keeps you one step ahead.

Embrace Technology: In today's digital age, being technologically savvy is like having a cheat code in the game of sales. From CRM software to social media platforms, leverage technology to streamline processes, gather insights, and connect with customers in innovative ways. Just think of it as leveling up your sales game with a power-up potion.

Customer-Centric Mindset: It's not just about selling products; it's about solving problems and meeting needs. Adopt a customer-centric approach that focuses on understanding their pain points, preferences, and evolving demands. Think of yourself as a sales Sherlock Holmes, constantly sleuthing for clues to better serve your customers.

Continuous Learning: The sales landscape is a bit like Hogwarts—there's always something new to learn. Whether it's honing your negotiation skills, mastering the art of storytelling, or delving into behavioral economics, commit to lifelong learning. Consider it your own personal "sales Hogwarts," where each new skill is a magical spell in your arsenal.

Adaptability Mindset: Finally, embrace adaptability as a mindset, not just a skill. Be open to change, resilient in the face of challenges, and agile in your approach. Remember, it's not about being the fastest or the strongest; it's about being the most adaptable—the MacGyver of sales, if you will.

So, there you have it—a crash course in adaptability in the sales landscape while keeping things light. Now, go forth and conquer the ever-evolving world of sales like a true sales ninja!

9. Integrity

Trust is the foundation of any successful sales relationship. Ethical salespeople prioritize honesty and transparency, even if it means sacrificing a short-term gain for the sake of long-term trust and reputation.

Integrity in Sales: Balancing Trust and Profit

Ah, the noble art of salesmanship! Picture this: a suave salesperson, clad in a sharp suit, armed not with gimmicks but with integrity. In sales, integrity reigns supreme. It's the cornerstone upon which enduring relationships between sellers and buyers are built. But how does one navigate this labyrinth of ethical dilemmas while still sealing the deal? Fear not, for we shall embark on this academic adventure together, armed with wit and wisdom.

The Foundation of Trust

Trust, like a delicate soufflé, takes time and effort to rise but can collapse with the slightest mishap. Ethical salespeople understand this fundamental truth. They prioritize honesty and transparency, even when faced with the tantalizing allure of short-term gains. Imagine a salesperson faced with a choice: inflate the benefits of a product to close a sale or provide honest, realistic information. The ethical warrior opts for the latter, knowing that a foundation built on truth will weather the storms of doubt and scrutiny.

Examples from the Trenches

Consider the case of Joe, a seasoned sales executive. Joe encounters a potential client eager to sign a contract for a product that doesn't entirely meet their needs. Instead of glossing over the shortcomings, Joe takes a different approach. He lays bare the limitations of the product, offering alternative solutions that better align with the client's requirements. While this may seem like a risky gambit, Joe understands that trust is the currency of sustainable business relationships. His honesty pays dividends in the long run, earning him not just a sale but a loyal advocate for his brand.

Tips for Cultivating Integrity in Sales

Now, dear reader, you may wonder, how does one cultivate this elusive trait of integrity in the cutthroat world of sales? Fear not, for I shall impart upon you some pearls of wisdom.

- ✓ **Know Thy Product:** Familiarize yourself with the ins and outs of what you're selling. Honesty thrives in the soil of knowledge.
- ✓ **Listen, Don't Just Hear:** Integrity is about how well you understand your client's needs. You show respect when you genuinely listen, and a commitment to finding the right solution rather than just making a sale.
- ✓ **Underpromise, Overdeliver:** Set realistic expectations and then exceed them. Your clients will appreciate the pleasant surprise.
- ✓ **Embrace Transparency:** Be forthright about any limitations or drawbacks of your product. Transparency breeds trust.
- ✓ **Long-Term Vision:** Remember, it's not just about closing the deal today but building relationships that endure beyond the transaction. This brings in dedicated clients who remain with you.

In the grand tapestry of salesmanship, integrity stands as a beacon of light, guiding us through the murky waters of temptation and deceit. Armed with honesty and transparency, we embark on our quest to forge lasting relationships built on trust. So go forth, dear reader, and may your sales be as ethical as they are successful!

10. Goal Orientation

Setting and working toward clear, achievable goals is crucial for maintaining focus and motivation in sales. Great salespeople are driven by targets and continuously strive to exceed them.

Understanding Goal Orientation

In the dynamic world of sales, setting clear and attainable objectives serves as the compass guiding a salesperson through the tumultuous seas of customer interactions and negotiations. Imagine a ship without a destination; it would aimlessly drift, at the mercy of unpredictable currents. Similarly, a salesperson without defined goals risks wandering aimlessly in the vast ocean of opportunities.

Examples of Goal Orientation

Consider a sales representative tasked with increasing the quarterly revenue by 20%. Armed with this goal, they meticulously strategize their approach. They identify potential clients, tailor pitches to address specific needs, and diligently follow up on leads. With each successful sale, they edge closer to their target, spurred on by the thrill of progress.

Or picture a sales team competing in a friendly rivalry to secure the highest number of new accounts. Motivated by the desire to outperform their colleagues, each member channels their energies into prospecting, nurturing relationships, and sealing deals. The camaraderie fosters healthy competition, driving the team toward collective success.

Tips to Develop Goal Orientation

- ✓ **Define Clear Objectives:** Like a scholar outlining a thesis statement, articulate your sales objectives with precision. Ambiguity breeds confusion, while clarity fuels purposeful action.
- ✓ **Break Goals into Bite-sized Chunks:** Tackling a mammoth goal can be overwhelming. Divide it into smaller, manageable tasks akin to dissecting a complex theory into digestible concepts.
- ✓ **Track Progress:** Just as a scholar monitors their research milestones, diligently track your sales progress. Celebrate victories, learn from setbacks, and adjust strategies accordingly.
- ✓ **Seek Feedback:** Embrace constructive criticism as eagerly as a student welcomes feedback on their dissertation. Solicit input from mentors, peers, and customers to refine your approach.
- ✓ **Stay Flexible:** While steadfastness is admirable, adaptability is indispensable. Like a scholar revising their hypotheses in light of new evidence, be willing to pivot your sales strategies as circumstances evolve.
- ✓ **Visualize Success:** Envision yourself achieving your sales goals with the clarity of a scholar visualizing their name on the cover of a published paper. Harness the power of visualization to fuel your determination.
- ✓ **Maintain Discipline:** Just as scholarly pursuits demand unwavering discipline, so do your sales routines. Consistent effort compounds over time, propelling you closer to your objectives.

In essence, embodying goal orientation in sales is akin to embarking on an academic quest—guided by clear objectives, fueled by relentless determination, and enriched by the wisdom gleaned from both successes and failures. So, don your metaphorical cap and gown, fellow sales scholar, and let the pursuit of lofty goals be your academic odyssey!

3

FROM ROLODEX TO CRM—NAVIGATING THE SALES ODYSSEY

In the annals of sales history, my journey from lead generation to closure has been a fascinating adventure. Imagine me, armed with a trusty Rolodex and a charming smile, navigating through what seemed like a labyrinthine maze. Fast forward to today, and technology reigns supreme, transforming the sales process into a finely tuned symphony of digital wizardry and human finesse. Join me as I take you through the epochs of sales, comparing the antiquated methods of the early 90s to the dynamic landscape of contemporary salesmanship.

Ah, the amusing world of modern sales! While many salespeople today are up to speed with all the latest tricks and changes, I'm here to write for folks like me who've been in the game a while and might need a little catch-up. This chapter is our guide, tailored to help us seasoned leaders navigate the twists and turns of this ever-evolving landscape. But hold on, our journey doesn't stop here! There's another chapter ahead, filled with tips on how to get involved in online communities and a chapter on how to become a better leader. As the wise Socrates once said, "The secret of change is to focus all of your energy not on fighting the old, but on building the new." So, let's dive into this adventure together, ready to learn and grow along the way!

1. Lead Generation: My Quest for the Holy Grail

In the early 90s, I was the sales rep armed with a stack of business cards, attending networking events and trade shows in search of the elusive golden lead. Cold calling was my daily routine, hoping for a warm reception amidst countless rejections. But today, I harness the power of inbound marketing and social media sleuthing. With data analytics and AI algorithms at my disposal, I pinpoint potential leads with surgical precision. LinkedIn has become my modern-day oracle, revealing hidden gems amidst the digital cacophony.

Evolution and Techniques

Lead generation is a crucial aspect of marketing that involves identifying and attracting potential customers for a business's products or services. Over time, the methods and techniques for lead generation have evolved significantly, driven by changes in technology, consumer behavior, and market dynamics. Let's explore the evolution of lead generation techniques from traditional methods to modern strategies.

Traditional Lead Generation Techniques

Cold Calling: Historically, cold calling was a prevalent method for generating leads. Sales representatives would contact prospects over the phone without any prior interaction, aiming to spark interest in the product or service.

Direct Mail: Sending physical mail, such as brochures, flyers, and catalogs to potential customers' addresses was another traditional lead generation technique. While this method could be costly and time-consuming, it allowed businesses to reach a targeted audience.

Print Advertising: Placing advertisements in newspapers, magazines, and other printed publications was a common way to generate leads. Advertisements could be targeted based on the publication's audience demographics.

Trade Shows and Events: Participating in trade shows, industry conferences, and networking events provided businesses with opportunities to showcase their products or services and connect with potential customers face to face.

Referral Programs: Encouraging existing customers to refer friends, family, or colleagues to the business was an effective way to generate leads through word-of-mouth marketing.

Modern Lead Generation Techniques

Content Marketing: Content marketing involves creating and distributing valuable, relevant content to attract and engage a target audience. Techniques such as blogging, video marketing, and social media content help businesses establish authority in their industry and attract leads organically.

Search Engine Optimization (SEO): SEO techniques aim to improve a website's visibility in search engine results, making it easier for potential customers to find business online. By optimizing website content, using relevant keywords, and earning backlinks from authoritative sources, businesses can attract organic traffic and generate leads.

Email Marketing: Email marketing remains a powerful lead generation tool, allowing businesses to nurture relationships with prospects and convert them into customers over time. Personalized email campaigns, automated drip sequences, and lead magnets (such as eBooks or webinars) help businesses capture the leads' contact information and deliver targeted messages.

Social Media Marketing: Social media platforms provide businesses with opportunities to engage with their target audience, build brand awareness, and generate leads. By sharing valuable content, running targeted advertising campaigns, and actively engaging with followers, businesses can attract leads and drive conversions.

Pay-Per-Click (PPC) Advertising: PPC advertising allows businesses to bid on keywords and display ads on search engines and social media platforms. By targeting specific keywords and demographics, businesses can drive targeted traffic to their websites and capture leads through landing pages or contact forms.

Marketing Automation: Marketing automation platforms enable businesses to streamline lead generation and nurture processes by automating repetitive tasks such as email campaigns, lead scoring, and CRM integration. By implementing marketing automation, businesses can effectively manage leads at scale and improve conversion rates.

Thus, traditional lead generation techniques laid the foundation for modern marketing practices, but businesses must adapt to changing trends and embrace digital strategies to remain competitive and effectively reach their target audience in today's digital age. The evolution of lead generation reflects broader shifts in consumer behavior and technological advancements. Traditional methods like cold calling and direct mail are still relevant in some industries but have become less effective due to changes in consumer preferences and the rise of digital marketing channels.

Modern lead generation techniques leverage the power of the internet, data analytics, and automation to reach and engage with prospects more effectively. By focusing on providing value, building relationships, and delivering personalized experiences, businesses can generate high-quality leads and drive sustainable growth in today's competitive marketplace.

2. Prospecting: Mining for Gems

In the past, I embarked on the arduous task of prospecting where hours were spent dialing numbers, hoping for a nibble on the other end of the line. But today, with the advent of Customer Relationship Management (CRM) systems, prospecting has transformed into a veritable treasure hunt. Automated lead scoring algorithms sift through mountains of data, identifying high-value prospects with laser-like accuracy. Predictive analytics now empower me to foresee potential opportunities before they even materialize.

Evolution and Techniques

Prospecting has evolved dramatically from its traditional roots, with modern techniques proving to be significantly more efficient and impactful, largely due to advancements in technology. While methods like cold calling, networking events, and direct mail once formed the foundation of sales outreach, they were often time-consuming, geographically limited, and difficult to measure in terms of return on investment. Today, however, sales professionals have access to powerful digital tools that streamline and enhance the prospecting process. Social media platforms like LinkedIn and Twitter enable highly targeted outreach and direct engagement with decision-makers, while email marketing automation allows for personalized, scalable communication supported by real-time analytics. Content marketing, combined with search engine optimization (SEO), helps attract inbound leads by offering valuable and relevant content to potential customers actively searching for solutions. Additionally, the integration of Customer Relationship Management (CRM) systems with sales intelligence tools provides a data-driven approach to prospecting, enabling lead scoring, predictive analytics, and effective prioritization. Together, these modern techniques not only improve accessibility and reach but also significantly boost the effectiveness of prospecting efforts, making them indispensable in today's competitive sales environment.

Comparison

The evolution of prospecting from traditional to modern methods has brought about significant changes in terms of *accessibility, efficiency, and effectiveness.* While traditional techniques like cold calling and direct mail are still utilized to some extent, they are often complemented or replaced by digital strategies that leverage the power of technology.

Accessibility: Modern prospecting techniques, enabled by technology, offer greater accessibility to a wider pool of potential prospects. Social media platforms, email marketing automation, and content marketing allow businesses to reach audiences across geographical boundaries and engage with them on their preferred channels.

Efficiency: Modern techniques leverage automation, data analytics, and AI-driven insights to streamline the prospecting process, allowing sales teams to focus their efforts on the most promising leads and opportunities.

Effectiveness: Advanced techniques prioritize quality over quantity unlike traditional methods that relied on volume and repetition. By leveraging data-driven insights and personalized communication strategies, businesses can build deeper relationships with prospects and deliver more relevant solutions, ultimately driving higher conversion rates and ROI.

So, it is safe to say that the transformative impact of technology on sales and marketing practices is dynamic and efficient providing greater accessibility, efficiency, and effectiveness in identifying and cultivating potential customers in today's digital age. Embracing these advancements and adapting to changing consumer behaviors is essential for businesses looking to thrive in a competitive marketplace.

3. Follow-up: The Art of Persistence

In the past, the follow-up dance was a delicate balance between tenacity and tact. I navigated the fine line between being perceived as a diligent professional and a pesky pest. Post-it notes adorned my cubicle walls, reminding me of pending callbacks and promised follow-ups. But today, with email automation and CRM reminders, follow-ups have evolved into a meticulously choreographed ballet.

The Evolution of Follow-up Techniques

Follow-up, as a practice, has long been an essential component in various fields such as sales, marketing, customer service, and even personal relationships. It serves the purpose of maintaining communication, reinforcing relationships, and ensuring that commitments are fulfilled. Over time, the techniques and methods of follow-up have evolved significantly, primarily driven by technological advancements.

Traditional Follow-up Techniques

Phone Calls: In the pre-digital age, phone calls were the primary mode of follow-up. Sales representatives, for instance, would diligently dial numbers to reconnect with prospects, discuss proposals, or address concerns. While effective in establishing direct communication, this method was time-consuming and often relied heavily on the availability of both parties.

Face-to-Face Meetings: Another traditional approach involved face-to-face meetings, particularly common in industries where personal relationships were paramount, such as business-to-business sales. While effective for building rapport, these meetings were resource-intensive and limited by geographical constraints.

Postal Mail: Sending letters or postcards was a common way to follow up, especially in formal or professional contexts. However, the process was slow, lacked immediacy, and required physical resources for printing and postage.

Emails and Fax: As technology advanced, emails and fax machines became prevalent for follow-up. While faster than postal mail, emails still required a degree of patience, and fax machines had limitations in terms of document quality and reliability.

Modern Follow-up Techniques with Technology

Email Automation: With the advent of email automation software, follow-up emails can now be scheduled and personalized at scale. These platforms allow for segmentation, tracking, and analysis, significantly improving efficiency and effectiveness.

CRM Systems: Customer Relationship Management (CRM) systems have revolutionized follow-up in sales and marketing. These platforms centralize customer data, track interactions, and automate follow-up tasks, ensuring timely and personalized communication.

Social media: Platforms like LinkedIn, Twitter, and Facebook have become valuable tools for follow-up. Professionals can engage with prospects, share relevant content, and maintain ongoing conversations, all within a digital ecosystem.

Text Messaging and Chatbots: SMS and messaging apps have emerged as convenient channels for follow-up. Additionally, AI-powered chatbots can engage with leads or customers in real time, providing immediate assistance or routing inquiries to the appropriate personnel.

Video Conferencing: Virtual meetings through platforms like Zoom or Microsoft Teams have become increasingly popular for follow-up discussions. They offer the benefits of face-to-face interaction without the need for physical proximity, saving time and resources.

Mobile Apps: Many businesses now utilize mobile apps for follow-up purposes. These apps can send push notifications, provide updates, and facilitate transactions, offering a seamless and personalized user experience.

Comparison

The evolution of follow-up techniques from traditional to modern methods underscores the transformative power of technology. While traditional approaches like phone calls and face-to-face meetings remain relevant in certain contexts, modern tools and platforms have vastly expanded the possibilities for communication and relationship-building. Modern follow-up techniques offer several advantages over their traditional counterparts. They are often faster, more scalable, and provide greater flexibility in terms of timing and personalization. Moreover, digital follow-up methods enable better tracking and analysis, allowing organizations to measure engagement metrics and refine their strategies accordingly.

However, it's essential to recognize that technology is not a panacea. While it enhances efficiency and accessibility, it cannot replace the human touch entirely. Effective follow-up still requires empathy, authenticity, and a genuine commitment to building relationships.

Embracing modern tools while staying true to timeless principles, organizations can optimize their follow-up efforts and cultivate lasting connections in an increasingly digital world.

4. Managing the Sales Cycle: My Juggling Act

The sales cycle is the step-by-step journey a potential customer takes—from the first point of contact to closing the deal. It typically includes stages like prospecting, qualifying leads, presenting solutions, handling objections, negotiating, and finalizing the sale. In other words, it's the full process of turning interest into commitment.

In the earlier days, sales cycles resembled a chaotic circus act, with me juggling an assortment of leads, proposals, and negotiations. Excel spreadsheets served as my makeshift ringmaster, attempting to corral disparate data into a semblance of order.

But today, the game has changed. With modern CRM platforms, AI-driven insights, and workflow automation, the sales cycle has become far more streamlined and strategic. Sales teams now get real-time visibility into deals, can prioritize efforts based on predictive analytics, and automate repetitive tasks—freeing up time to focus on what matters most: closing the deal.

Evolution and Techniques

Sales, often dubbed as the lifeblood of any business, has undergone a significant transformation over the years. From traditional face-to-face interactions to leveraging cutting-edge technologies, managing the sales cycle has evolved to meet the demands of a rapidly changing market landscape.

Traditional Techniques

Traditionally, managing the sales cycle revolved around personal relationships, cold calls, and physical sales pitches. Sales representatives would spend hours on the road, visiting potential clients and engaging in lengthy negotiations. The process was often slow, labor-intensive, and heavily reliant on individual charisma and persuasion skills.

Manual Prospecting: In the past, sales professionals relied heavily on manual prospecting techniques such as cold calling, door-to-door visits, and networking events. This process was time-consuming and often yielded limited results, requiring significant effort to identify potential leads.

Face-to-Face Meetings: Building rapport and trust with clients necessitated face-to-face interactions. Sales representatives would travel extensively to meet prospects, understand their needs, and tailor solutions accordingly. While effective, this approach was resource-intensive and constrained by geographical limitations.

Paper-Based Documentation: Contracts, proposals, and other sales documents were predominantly paper-based. Managing and tracking these documents required meticulous attention to detail, often resulting in delays and errors.

Limited Data Analysis: Analyzing sales data was challenging due to the absence of sophisticated analytics tools. Sales managers relied on manual reporting methods, making it difficult to gain actionable insights and optimize strategies effectively.

Modern Evolution with Technology

The advent of technology has revolutionized the sales cycle, empowering organizations to streamline processes, enhance productivity, and drive revenue growth. With the proliferation of digital tools and platforms, sales professionals now have unprecedented access to data, automation, and analytics capabilities.

Digital Prospecting: Today, sales teams leverage advanced CRM software and data analytics tools to identify and prioritize leads. Automated lead scoring algorithms help sales representatives focus their efforts on high-potential prospects, significantly improving efficiency and effectiveness.

Virtual Selling: The rise of virtual communication platforms such as Zoom, Microsoft Teams, and Slack have transformed the way sales interactions take place. Remote selling allows sales professionals to engage with clients from anywhere in the world, eliminating geographical barriers and enabling faster deal closures.

Electronic Documentation: Paper-based documentation has been replaced by digital contracts, e-signatures, and cloud-based collaboration tools. Sales teams can now create, share, and track documents in real time, streamlining the negotiation process and reducing administrative overhead.

Advanced Analytics: Modern CRM platforms offer robust analytics capabilities, allowing sales managers to gain deeper insights into customer behavior, sales performance, and market trends. Predictive analytics algorithms help forecast future sales opportunities, enabling proactive decision-making and strategy refinement.

In conclusion, the evolution of managing the sales cycle from traditional techniques to modern-day practices has been marked by a seismic shift in approach, driven largely by technological advancements. While traditional methods emphasized personal relationships and manual processes, the accessibility to technology has ushered in a new era of efficiency, scalability, and data-driven decision-making. By embracing digital tools and leveraging data analytics, organizations can navigate the complexities of the modern sales landscape with confidence and agility, ultimately driving sustainable growth and competitive advantage.

5. Negotiation and Closure: Sealing the Deal

Back in the days, negotiation was a high-stakes game of poker, with both parties bluffing and counterbluffing in a bid for supremacy. Handshakes were exchanged, contracts were signed, and victory cigars were lit amidst a haze of uncertainty. But today, negotiation has transformed into a collaborative dance, facilitated by video conferencing and virtual deal rooms. E-signature tools streamline the paperwork process, expediting closure with a few clicks of a mouse. We leverage data-driven insights to tailor proposals, ensuring a win-win outcome for all parties involved.

Evolution and Techniques

Negotiation and closure are two critical components in various aspects of life, whether in business dealings, interpersonal relationships, or even political diplomacy. Both processes involve reaching agreements or resolutions, but they operate in distinct ways, each with its own set of techniques and strategies. Over time, these techniques have evolved, especially with the advent and accessibility of technology, altering the landscape of negotiation and closure.

Traditional Techniques

Negotiation

Positional Bargaining: This traditional technique involves parties taking extreme positions and gradually compromising to reach a mutually acceptable agreement.

Win-Lose Mentality: Often characterized by adversarial approaches, one party seeks to gain at the expense of the other.

Limited Information Sharing: Parties tend to withhold information to maintain leverage during negotiations.

Face-to-Face Meetings: Direct interaction between parties is common, allowing for non-verbal cues and body language to play a significant role in communication.

Closure

Formal Agreements: Closure often involves formalizing agreements reached during negotiations through contracts, treaties, or other legal documents.

Clear Terms and Conditions: The terms of closure are explicitly outlined, leaving little room for ambiguity or misunderstanding.

Finality: Closure implies the conclusion of a particular matter, signaling that all parties have fulfilled their obligations or reached a resolution.

Verification and Compliance: Ensuring that both parties adhere to the terms of the agreement is crucial for closure, often involving mechanisms for verification and enforcement.

Modern Evolution

Negotiation

Interest-Based Negotiation: Modern negotiation techniques focus on identifying underlying interests rather than entrenched positions, fostering collaboration and creative problem-solving.

Principled Negotiation: Introduced by Fisher and Ury in their book *Getting to Yes*, this approach emphasizes separating people from the problem, focusing on interests, generating options for mutual gain, and insisting on objective criteria.

Information Sharing and Transparency: With the rise of transparency and information accessibility, parties are more inclined to share relevant data openly, fostering trust and enhancing the quality of negotiations.

Virtual Negotiations: Technology has facilitated virtual negotiations through video conferencing and collaborative platforms, enabling parties to negotiate across geographical boundaries efficiently.

Closure

Electronic Signatures and Digital Contracts: The advent of electronic signatures and digital contracts has streamlined the closure process, allowing parties to finalize agreements remotely and expedite the signing process.

Blockchain Technology: Blockchain technology offers immutable records of transactions, enhancing the security and transparency of closure processes, particularly in financial and legal domains.

Automated Compliance Monitoring: AI-driven tools can monitor and enforce compliance with contractual obligations, reducing the need for manual oversight and ensuring smoother closure procedures.

Data Analytics for Performance Evaluation: Organizations leverage data analytics to evaluate the performance of agreements post-closure, identifying areas for improvement and optimizing future negotiations.

As technology continues to advance, the evolution of negotiation and closure processes is likely to persist, shaping the way individuals and organizations approach agreements and their subsequent conclusions. Adaptation to these changes is essential for stakeholders to navigate the complexities of negotiation and achieve effective closure in an ever-evolving landscape.

As I bid adieu to the bygone era of Rolodexes and phone books, I stand at the precipice of a brave new world of salesmanship. The journey from lead generation to closure has undergone a metamorphosis, driven by technological innovation and a relentless pursuit of excellence. Yet, amidst the ever-changing landscape of sales, one thing remains constant: the timeless art of human connection. So, as I move along on my own sales odyssey, I remember to wield technology as a tool, but never forget the power of a genuine smile and a firm handshake.

6. Customer Feedback: Navigating Customer Satisfaction in Sales

In the early days of my career, feedback and gauging customer satisfaction felt like a labyrinthine quest. Armed with little more than pen and paper, I sought out insights amidst the cacophony of opinions, hoping to uncover the elusive golden nuggets of feedback. Surveys and face-to-face conversations were my tools, navigating through the maze of varied responses and interpretations. Cold calls were not just about pitching but also about understanding the pulse of the customer base. But today, I harness the power of technology and data analytics, employing sophisticated feedback mechanisms and sentiment analysis tools. Through AI algorithms, I sift through mountains of data to pinpoint trends and glean actionable insights. Social media platforms serve as modern-day oracles, offering real-time feedback and direct communication channels with customers.

LinkedIn, in particular, has become a treasure trove of opinions and sentiments, revealing hidden gems amidst the digital noise.

The Evolution of Customer Feedback Collection and Experience Measurement

Gathering customer feedback and measuring their experience has long been crucial for businesses across various industries. Understanding customer sentiments, preferences, and pain points not only allows companies to improve their products and services but also fosters stronger customer relationships. Over time, the methods and tools for collecting feedback and measuring customer experience have evolved significantly, driven primarily by technological advancements. In this comprehensive comparison, we'll explore the traditional techniques of gathering customer feedback and how they've evolved in the modern era with the accessibility of technology.

Traditional Feedback Collection Techniques

Surveys: Traditional surveys, whether conducted over the phone, through postal mail, or in-person, were a common method for gathering customer feedback. While surveys provided valuable insights, they were often time-consuming to administer and had relatively low response rates.

Focus Groups: Another traditional approach involved convening focus groups to discuss products, services, or experiences. While focus groups allowed for in-depth discussions and qualitative feedback, they were limited in scale and could be influenced by group dynamics.

Comment Cards: Businesses often distributed comment cards in physical locations such as retail stores or restaurants, allowing customers to provide feedback directly. However, this method lacked anonymity and might not capture feedback from a broader customer base.

One-on-One Interviews: Personal interviews with customers provided detailed qualitative feedback but were resource-intensive and limited in scalability.

Modern Feedback Collection Techniques with Technology

Online Surveys: The advent of online survey platforms has revolutionized feedback collection, making it easier to reach a larger audience and analyze responses efficiently. These platforms offer customizable survey templates, real-time analytics, and automated follow-up.

Social Media Monitoring: Social media platforms like Twitter, Facebook, and Instagram serve as valuable channels for gathering customer feedback in real time. Through social listening tools, businesses can track mentions, hashtags, and comments to understand customer sentiment and address issues promptly.

Feedback Widgets and Pop-ups: Many websites and mobile apps now incorporate feedback widgets or pop-ups to solicit user feedback at various touchpoints. These tools offer a non-intrusive way for customers to share their thoughts and experiences.

Net Promoter Score (NPS): NPS surveys have gained popularity as a simple yet effective way to measure customer satisfaction and loyalty. By asking a single question ("How likely are you to recommend us to a friend or colleague?"), businesses can gauge overall customer sentiment and identify areas for improvement.

Online Reviews and Ratings: Platforms like Yelp, TripAdvisor, and Google Reviews enable customers to leave feedback and ratings, providing valuable insights for businesses while also influencing purchasing decisions for other potential customers.

Artificial Intelligence (AI) and Sentiment Analysis: AI-powered tools can analyze large volumes of unstructured data, such as customer reviews or social media posts, to identify trends, sentiment, and emerging issues automatically.

Comparison

The evolution of customer feedback collection techniques from traditional to modern methods highlights the transformative impact of technology. While traditional approaches like surveys and focus groups remain relevant, modern tools and platforms offer several advantages. They are often more scalable, accessible, and provide real-time insights for timely action. Moreover, modern feedback collection methods leverage the power of data analytics and AI to uncover hidden patterns and sentiments, enabling businesses to make more informed decisions and prioritize improvements effectively. However, it's essential to recognize that technology alone is not sufficient. Effective feedback collection requires proactive engagement, active listening, and a genuine commitment to addressing customer needs and concerns.

You can see that customer feedback collection techniques underscore the importance of adapting to technological advancements while maintaining a customer-centric approach. By leveraging modern tools and platforms while embracing timeless principles of customer satisfaction, businesses can enhance their understanding of customer needs and ultimately drive long-term success in an increasingly competitive landscape.

7. Unveiling Upselling and Cross-Selling Treasures: Navigating Sales Expansion Opportunities

In the past, identifying upselling and cross-selling opportunities felt like searching for hidden treasure—reliant on gut instinct and lucky breaks. Valuable chances were often buried in routine interactions, overlooked amid daily demands. Today, advanced analytics and predictive modeling have replaced guesswork, allowing sales teams to pinpoint these opportunities with accuracy. Every transaction and customer behavior is mined to reveal patterns that highlight what additional value we can offer. With tools like LinkedIn enabling strategic touchpoints, upselling and cross-selling have evolved from opportunistic to intentional—turning standard deals into deeper, more profitable partnerships.

The Evolution of Upselling and Cross-Selling

Identifying upselling and cross-selling opportunities with existing customers has long been a cornerstone of effective sales and marketing strategies. These techniques not only drive revenue growth but also deepen customer relationships by offering tailored solutions and additional value. Over time, the methods and tools for identifying such opportunities have evolved significantly, largely due to advancements in technology and data analytics. In this comprehensive comparison, we'll explore the traditional techniques of identifying upselling and cross-selling opportunities, and how they've evolved in the modern era with the accessibility of technology.

Traditional Techniques for Identifying Upselling and Cross-Selling Opportunities

Personalized Sales Interactions: In the past, sales representatives relied heavily on personal relationships and face-to-face interactions to identify upselling and cross-selling opportunities. By understanding customers' needs and preferences through ongoing conversations, salespeople could suggest relevant additional products or services.

Manual Data Analysis: Traditional methods often involved manual analysis of customer data, such as purchase history and demographics, to identify patterns and opportunities. While effective to some extent, this approach was time-consuming and lacked real-time insights.

Customer Surveys and Feedback: Businesses would often conduct surveys or seek feedback from customers to understand their preferences and identify potential upselling or cross-selling opportunities. However, this method relied on customers voluntarily providing information and did not always capture all relevant data points.

Retail Merchandising and Product Placement: In retail settings, strategic merchandising and product placement were used to encourage impulse purchases and cross-selling. While effective for increasing average transaction value, this approach was limited by physical constraints.

Modern Techniques for Identifying Upselling and Cross-Selling Opportunities with Technology

Data Analytics and Machine Learning: The advent of advanced data analytics and machine learning algorithms has transformed upselling and cross-selling strategies. By analyzing vast amounts of customer data, including transaction history, browsing behavior, and social media interactions, businesses can identify patterns and predict future purchasing behavior with greater accuracy.

Recommendation Engines: Many e-commerce platforms utilize recommendation engines powered by AI to suggest relevant products or services based on customers' past behavior and preferences. These personalized recommendations increase the likelihood of upsells and cross-sells.

Customer Segmentation: CRM systems and marketing automation tools enable businesses to segment their customer base into distinct groups based on various criteria, such as purchase history, demographics, or psychographics. By tailoring marketing messages and offers to specific segments, businesses can effectively identify upselling and cross-selling opportunities.

Predictive Analytics: Predictive analytics tools leverage historical data and statistical algorithms to forecast future trends and identify potential upselling or cross-selling opportunities. These insights enable businesses to proactively target customers with relevant offers at the right time.

Dynamic Pricing Strategies: Dynamic pricing algorithms adjust product prices in real time based on factors such as demand, inventory levels, and customer segments. By offering personalized pricing incentives, businesses can encourage upsells and cross-sells.

Integration with Customer Service Channels: Integrating sales and customer service channels allows businesses to identify upselling and cross-selling opportunities during customer interactions. For example, customer service representatives can recommend complementary products or services based on customers' inquiries or support requests.

Comparison

The evolution of techniques for identifying upselling and cross-selling opportunities reflects the increasing importance of data-driven insights and personalized interactions in sales and marketing. While traditional approaches like personal sales interactions and merchandising tactics remain relevant, modern tools and technologies offer unprecedented capabilities for understanding customer behavior and preferences. Moreover, modern techniques enable businesses to leverage automation and AI to scale their upselling and cross-selling efforts effectively. However, it's essential to balance data-driven insights with human intuition and empathy. Effective upselling and cross-selling require a deep understanding of customers' needs and preferences as well as the ability to anticipate their future requirements.

So, there you are. By embracing technology and leveraging customer data effectively, businesses can unlock new revenue streams and foster stronger relationships with existing customers in an increasingly competitive marketplace.

My Evolution Continues: As I bid adieu to the bygone era, I stand at the precipice of a brave new world of salesmanship. The journey from lead generation to closure has undergone a metamorphosis, driven by technological innovation and a relentless pursuit of excellence. Yet, amidst the ever-changing landscape of sales, one thing remains constant: the timeless art of human connection. So, as I move along on my own sales odyssey, I remember to wield technology as a tool, but never forget the power of a genuine smile and a firm handshake.

4

STEERING MODERN SALESMANSHIP

Before delving into the next chapter of this book, I wanted to recount my latest experience to emphasize the significance of incorporating online strategies and modern techniques in your sales endeavors.

So then, picture, if you will, a seasoned sales maestro is thrust into the tumultuous world of a technology startup. But this was no ordinary startup; it was a bootstrapped venture, teeming with revolutionary potential yet shackled by financial constraints.

In this narrative, I wasn't leading a seasoned sales army—I was a lone adventurer, equipped with cutting-edge technology and a relentless drive to explore untapped markets. As the head of the technology sales team at a budding startup, I embarked on a mission to ignite sales growth from the ground up. Standing once again at the edge of the unknown, I honed the timeless crafts of direct selling and cold calling, blending tradition with innovation to chart a bold path forward.

Our product, a beacon of innovation in the form of an end-to-end retail planning platform, shimmered with promise. Yet, the specter of obscurity loomed large over us. Our brand? A mere whisper in the clamor of the market. Our clientele? A blank canvas, waiting to be painted with success. Our resources? Scarce, to say the least. But fear not, for where there's a will, there's always a way!

In that obscure scenario, the first step was to understand our product inside out, to grasp its nuances and its potential to transform the retail landscape. With this knowledge as my guide, I set out to identify our target market, meticulously researching industries ripe for innovation and disruption. But research alone wouldn't suffice; action was needed. So, I started cold calling, dialing numbers with precision and conviction.

Yet, I knew that direct selling could only take us so far. To truly make a mark in the industry, we needed to amplify our presence. And so, I leveraged the power of networking and forging alliances with key players in the retail ecosystem. Every handshake, every exchange of business cards, was a step closer to our goal. Building social capital became an inevitable part of my strategy. Through genuine interactions and fostering relationships, we gained trust and credibility within the industry. This social currency opened doors that might have otherwise remained closed, paving the way for collaboration and mutual growth. But perhaps the most crucial aspect of our journey was adaptability. As the market evolved and new challenges emerged, so did our approach. I experimented with different sales tactics, refining my pitch based on feedback and market trends. And as my efforts began to bear fruit, momentum grew.

Now, dear readers, let me briefly outline my approach to handling this challenge, along with some valuable tips that might help you.

Know Your Product: Understanding your product inside out is paramount. It's not just about knowing its features but understanding how it solves real problems for your potential clients.

Identify Your Target Market: Research industries that are ripe for innovation and disruption. Tailor your approach to fit the needs of your potential clients within these industries.

Embrace Cold Calling: While it may seem daunting, cold calling can be an effective way to make initial connections. Be prepared, be confident, and focus on building a rapport rather than just selling.

Leverage Networking: Forge alliances with key players in your industry. Attend networking events, conferences, and seminars to expand your reach and build valuable relationships.

Build Social Capital: Genuine interactions and fostering relationships are key. Focus on building trust and credibility within your industry, as this can open doors to collaboration and growth.

Adaptability is Key: Stay agile and adaptable. The market is constantly evolving, so be ready to pivot your approach based on feedback and emerging trends.

Diving into Databases

Envision me, if you will, donning a virtual diving suit, plunging headlong into the vast ocean of data. With the aid of premier database providers and sophisticated automation tools, I meticulously curated email templates that would serve as the harbingers of our message. Through drip campaigns, carefully orchestrated to tantalize and engage, we cast our nets wide in search of potential prospects.

Tips to Effectively Utilize These Tools

Using database tools for prospecting can greatly enhance your ability to identify potential customers or clients. Here are some tips to effectively utilize these tools.

Define Your Target Audience: Before diving into database tools, clearly define the characteristics of your ideal customers. Consider factors such as demographics, industry, company size, location, and purchasing behavior.

Choose the Right Database Tool: There are various database tools available, each with its own features and capabilities. Some popular ones include Salesforce, HubSpot, ZoomInfo, LinkedIn Sales Navigator, and Clearbit. Choose a tool that aligns with your prospecting goals and budget. Use their advanced search filters to target prospects who closely match your ideal customer profile.

Segment Your Prospects: Divide your prospects into different segments based on common characteristics. This allows you to tailor your messaging and approach to each segment, increasing the likelihood of success.

Stay Updated with Real-Time Data: Regularly update your database with real-time data to ensure accuracy. You will avoid reaching out to outdated or irrelevant contacts.

Integrate with CRM Software: If you're using the CRM software, ensure that your database tool integrates seamlessly with it. This allows for smooth data transfer and ensures that all prospecting activities are tracked and managed efficiently.

Personalize Your Outreach: Use the information gathered from the database tool to personalize your outreach efforts. Reference specific details about the prospect's company or industry in your communications to demonstrate that you've done your research.

Track and Analyze Performance: Monitor the performance of your prospecting efforts using metrics such as response rates, conversion rates, and sales generated. Analyze this data to identify what's working well and areas for improvement.

Continuously Refine Your Approach: Prospect databases are dynamic, so it's essential to continuously refine your prospecting approach based on feedback and results. Experiment with different messaging, targeting criteria, and outreach strategies to optimize your efforts.

Stay Compliant with Data Regulations: Ensure that you comply with data privacy regulations such as GDPR and CCPA when using database tools for prospecting. Only collect and use data that is obtained ethically and with the prospect's consent.

By following these tips, you can effectively leverage database tools for prospecting and increase your chances of success in acquiring new customers or clients.

The Quest for Early Adopters

Like a modern-day Odysseus, I embarked on a quest through the digital realms of LinkedIn in search of our early adopters.

The quest for early adopters is a crucial phase in the lifecycle of any new product or innovation. Early adopters are adventurous individuals or organizations who are willing to try out new technologies, products, or services before they become mainstream. Securing early adopters can provide valuable feedback, help refine the product, generate initial buzz, and establish credibility in the market. Here are some tips for successfully finding and engaging early adopters.

Identify Your Target Audience: Understand who your ideal early adopters are. Consider demographics, psychographics, and behaviors that align with your product or innovation. Look for communities, forums, or social media groups where these individuals congregate.

Leverage Your Network: Tap into your personal and professional networks to find potential early adopters. Reach out to influencers, industry experts, or colleagues who may be interested in what you're offering. Utilize platforms like LinkedIn or attend industry events to expand your network.

Create Compelling Messaging: Craft a clear and compelling message that communicates the value proposition of your product or innovation. Highlight the benefits and why early adopters should be interested. Your messaging should resonate with their needs, aspirations, or pain points.

Offer Early Access or Beta Testing: Provide early adopters with exclusive access to your product or innovation. Offer them the opportunity to be part of beta testing or pilot programs. This not only makes them feel special but also allows you to gather valuable feedback for improvement.

Engage in Thought Leadership: Position yourself or your company as a thought leader in your industry. Share insights, expertise, and perspectives through blog posts, webinars, podcasts, or speaking engagements. Establishing credibility can attract early adopters who trust your vision and leadership.

Incentivize Adoption: Offer incentives or rewards to early adopters for trying out your product or innovation. This could include discounts, freebies, or special access to future features. Make it worthwhile for them to take a chance on something new.

Listen and Iterate: Actively listen to feedback from early adopters and be open to making improvements based on their insights. Iterate quickly based on their suggestions to show that you value their input and are committed to delivering a high-quality experience.

Build a Community: Foster a sense of belonging and community among early adopters. Encourage them to share their experiences, provide testimonials, and engage with each other. A strong community can help amplify your message and attract more early adopters.

Showcase Success Stories: Highlight success stories of early adopters who have benefited from your product or innovation. Case studies, testimonials, or user-generated content can build credibility and inspire others to join the early adopter ranks.

Stay Agile and Adaptive: Be flexible and willing to adapt your strategy based on market feedback and evolving trends. The quest for early adopters is an ongoing process that requires continuous learning and adjustment.

These tips and strategies will enable you to effectively find and engage early adopters who will champion your product or innovation, paving the way for broader market adoption in the future.

LinkedIn Liaisons and Networking

Ah, LinkedIn, the hallowed halls of professional networking! Here, I danced a delicate ballet of connection requests and captivating content, all while showcasing our product through mesmerizing demos and captivating animations. With each post, each interaction, I sought to weave a narrative that would resonate with our audience, beckoning them to join us on our journey. (You will find more details on this in the next chapter.)

The Dance of Demos

With each demo, I embarked on a delicate pas de deux with potential clients, guiding them through the intricacies of our product with the finesse of a seasoned maestro. Armed with knowledge and passion, I sought not just to sell but to educate, to inspire, to ignite a spark of curiosity that would blossom into a lasting partnership. And lo and behold, after countless presentations and tireless efforts, our first client emerged from the fray, a beacon of hope in the stormy seas of sales.

The Importance of Product Demos in the Digital Age

Product demonstrations serve as the gateway to understanding and appreciating the value proposition of a product or service. As the world becomes increasingly digital, the significance of online demos escalates, serving as pivotal moments in the buyer's journey. These demos are not merely presentations; they are immersive experiences that can make or break a potential sale. Here's why they are crucial and some essential tips for delivering masterful demos:

1. Visualizing Functionality:

Product demos provide an opportunity for potential customers to visualize how the technology platform operates in real-world scenarios. Whether it's a software application, a cloud service, or a digital tool, seeing it in action helps users comprehend its functionalities, interface, and usability.

2. Building Trust:

In an era of online transactions and remote interactions, trust is paramount. A well-executed demo builds trust by showcasing the product's capabilities transparently. It demonstrates that the platform delivers what it promises, fostering confidence in its reliability and effectiveness.

3. Addressing Pain Points:

Effective demos tailor the presentation to address the specific pain points and needs of the audience. By highlighting how the technology platform can solve their challenges or improve their workflows, demos become personalized experiences that resonate with potential customers.

4. **Differentiating from Competitors:**

In a crowded marketplace, differentiation is key. A compelling demo not only showcases the unique features of the product but also articulates why it stands out from competitors. Demonstrating superior functionality, ease of use, or innovative solutions can sway decision-makers in your favor.

5. **Engaging the Audience:**

Online demos must captivate the audience's attention in a virtual environment where distractions abound. Utilize interactive elements, such as live demonstrations, polls, and Q&A sessions to keep participants engaged and actively involved in the presentation.

6. **Providing Value:**

A successful demo goes beyond product features; it demonstrates the value proposition and tangible benefits of the technology platform. Whether it is increasing efficiency, reducing costs, or enhancing productivity, emphasize how the product positively impacts the user's bottom line.

A check list that can help you:

- ✓ **Know Your Audience:** Tailor the demo to the needs, preferences, and pain points of the audience. Research their industry, challenges, and objectives to customize the presentation effectively.
- ✓ **Practice, Practice, Practice:** Familiarize yourself with the product inside out and rehearse the demo multiple times to

ensure a smooth and polished delivery. Anticipate potential questions or objections and prepare concise responses.

- ✓ **Keep It Concise:** Respect the audience's time by delivering a concise and focused demo. Highlight the most relevant features and benefits without overwhelming them with unnecessary details.
- ✓ **Tell a Compelling Story:** Frame the demo as a narrative that illustrates how the product solves a problem or fulfills a need. Use case studies, testimonials, or success stories to add credibility and resonance.
- ✓ **Be Interactive:** Encourage participation by inviting questions, soliciting feedback, and involving the audience in interactive activities. This fosters engagement and ensures that the demo is a two-way conversation rather than a one-sided presentation.
- ✓ **Follow Up:** After the demo, follow up promptly with additional information, answers to any outstanding questions, and next steps for further engagement or evaluation.

So, product demos play a pivotal role in showcasing the value proposition of technology platforms in the digital age. By delivering engaging, personalized, and value-driven presentations, you can effectively differentiate themselves, build trust, and convert prospects into satisfied customers.

Thus, amidst the exhilarating whirlwind of my sales odyssey, I found myself situated in Bangalore, India, a bustling hub of technological innovation. From this dynamic locale, I orchestrated a symphony of sales maneuvers that transcended geographical boundaries and spanned continents. Harnessing the power of modern communication technology, I seamlessly conducted product demonstrations via video calls to more than nine countries spread across the Americas, Europe, Singapore, the Middle East, and beyond. With each virtual interaction, I navigated the cultural nuances and time zone differences, forging connections with decision-makers and pitching our revolutionary retail planning platform with unwavering zeal.

It was during one such virtual encounter that fate smiled upon me from the desert sands of Dubai, UAE. In the shimmering metropolis of this global business hub, our first sale materialized, a testament to the efficacy of our approach and the universal appeal of our solution. So, as I reflect upon this remarkable journey, let it be known that our triumphs knew no bounds, transcending borders and uniting disparate corners of the globe under the banner of innovation and determination. From the vibrant streets of Bangalore to the cosmopolitan corridors of Dubai, our message resonated far and wide, heralding a new dawn in the realm of salesmanship.

And thus, dear reader, with one sale under our belt, our trajectory shifted forever. Through grit and wit we transcended obscurity and carved a niche in the annals of tech sales history. So, as I commit these words to paper, let them serve as a testament to the ever-evolving landscape of salesmanship. May my experiences illuminate your path, guiding you not only in sales techniques but also in the finer arts of management and leadership.

In the end, it's not just about overcoming challenges but embracing them as opportunities for growth and innovation. With passion, determination, and a strategic approach, even the most daunting of obstacles can be conquered.

5

STRATEGIES OF PARTICIPATING IN ONLINE COMMUNITIES

Allow me to describe a meticulously crafted strategy for immersing oneself in the arena of online communities and forums, where early adopters and prospects gather to share insights, participate in discussions, and demonstrate expertise across various domains.

- Prudently select online communities and forums frequented by early adopters, ensuring alignment with the subject matter at hand—retail planning and technology.
- Introduce oneself with finesse, articulating expertise and enthusiasm for the subject matter, thereby establishing credibility from the outset.
- Engage actively within the community by contributing insightful commentary, posing thought-provoking queries, and offering solutions to pertinent challenges.
- Cultivate relationships with fellow members through meaningful interactions, fostering a sense of camaraderie and mutual respect.
- Persistently demonstrate proficiency and innovation in the field, positioning oneself as a beacon of knowledge and ingenuity.

In the immortal words of Aristotle, "Excellence is never an accident. It is always the result of high intention, sincere effort, and intelligent execution." Thus, let us embark upon this odyssey of intellectual exchange and communal enrichment with zeal and sagacity.

Here's a step-by-step guide on how to implement the strategy of participating in online communities and forums:

1. Identify Relevant Communities and Forums

Look for online platforms where early adopters in the retail planning and technology space gather. This could include specialized forums, subreddits, LinkedIn groups, or industry-specific platforms.

- **Identify Your Target Audience:** Determine the specific demographic and interests of your target audience within the technology sector. Are you aiming to connect with tech executives, developers, or industry analysts? Knowing your audience will guide you to the most relevant communities.
- **Explore Industry-Specific Platforms:** Look for online platforms dedicated to the technology industry or tech enthusiasts. These platforms often have sections or groups focused on various aspects of sales in the tech sector. Examples include:
    - TechCrunch: A popular news and analysis website covering technology trends, startups, and innovation. It often features articles and discussions relevant to sales professionals in the tech industry.

- Sales Hacker: A community-driven platform offering resources, webinars, and discussions tailored to sales professionals, particularly in the tech sector.

Explore tech forums like Stack Overflow or GitHub Discussions, where tech professionals gather to ask questions, share insights, and discuss various topics, including sales strategies and techniques.

- **Utilize Social Media Channels:** Social media platforms such as LinkedIn, Twitter, and Facebook can be valuable for finding relevant communities and groups. Look for hashtags, groups, or pages related to sales in the tech industry. Examples include:
    - LinkedIn Groups: Join LinkedIn groups like "Tech Sales Professionals" or "SaaS Sales Strategies" to connect with peers and engage in discussions about sales in the tech sector.
    - Twitter or X Chats: Participate in Twitter chats focused on sales in technology by following relevant hashtags like #TechSales or #SaaS.

- **Explore Forums:** Explore forums like Reddit and other online forums which host communities covering a wide range of topics, including sales and technology. Look for subreddits or forums where discussions about sales in the tech industry occur. Examples include:
    - r/sales: A subreddit dedicated to discussions about sales strategies, techniques, and industry trends. While not specific to tech, it often features discussions relevant to sales professionals in the tech sector.

- Tech-focused Subreddits: Explore subreddits related to specific technologies or industries where sales professionals may gather to discuss sales-related topics.

- **Engage and Contribute:** Once you've identified relevant communities and forums, actively participate by asking questions, sharing insights, and engaging with other members. Building genuine relationships and providing value to the community will help you establish yourself as a trusted member.
- **Stay Updated:** Regularly check these platforms for new discussions, articles, and updates related to sales in the technology industry. Being actively involved in these communities will keep you informed about the latest trends and innovations, helping you stay ahead in the fast-paced tech sales landscape.

By following these steps and exploring the examples provided, you'll be able to identify and engage with relevant communities and forums in the technology sales space. Remember to approach these platforms with a mindset of learning, collaboration, and networking.

2. Research and Listen

Before jumping into discussions, spend some time observing the conversations already happening in these communities. Pay attention to the topics being discussed, the tone of the conversations, and the types of questions being asked. Researching and listening before engaging in discussions within communities is crucial for understanding the dynamics, norms, and expectations of those spaces. Here's a detailed breakdown with some useful tips.

- **Research**
  - **Identify Communities:** Determine which communities you're interested in joining or engaging with. These could be online forums, social media groups, subreddits, Discord servers, etc.
  - **Observe Platforms:** Understand the platforms where these communities exist. Each platform has its own culture and rules of engagement. For example, Reddit discussions tend to be more structured with threaded comments, while Twitter conversations are often more fast-paced and concise.
  - **Read Guidelines and Rules:** Most communities have rules and guidelines posted somewhere. Take the time to read and understand them to ensure you're following the community's expectations. Violating these rules can lead to your comments being deleted or even getting banned.
  - **Review Past Discussions:** Look through past discussions to get a sense of the topics that are commonly discussed, the prevailing opinions, and the overall tone of the community. This can give you valuable context before jumping in.
- **Listening**
  - **Observe Tone and Language:** Pay attention to the tone of conversations. Are they formal or informal? Is humor

prevalent? Understanding the tone helps you adjust your own communication style to fit in better.

- **Identify Key Contributors:** Take note of who the key contributors are within the community. These are the individuals who often drive discussions, provide valuable insights, or have significant influence. Observing their behavior can give you cues on how to engage effectively.
- **Identify Hot Topics:** Notice recurring themes or topics that generate a lot of discussion. These are likely areas where you can contribute meaningfully. However, be cautious about jumping into heated debates without understanding the context fully.
- **Note Unanswered Questions:** Look for questions or topics that haven't been adequately addressed. Providing thoughtful responses to these can establish your credibility within the community.

- **Tips**
  - **Start Slowly:** Don't rush into discussions immediately. Take some time to familiarize yourself with the community's dynamics before actively participating.
  - **Ask Clarifying Questions:** If you're unsure about something, ask clarifying questions to gain a better understanding. This shows that you're engaged and interested in learning from the community.
  - **Respect Diversity of Opinions:** Communities often comprise individuals with diverse backgrounds and viewpoints. Respect these differences even if you disagree,

and engage in constructive dialogue rather than resorting to confrontation.

- **Provide Value:** Aim to contribute value to the discussions. Share your expertise, provide helpful resources or insights, and offer support to other members when appropriate.

By researching and listening attentively before engaging, you'll be better equipped to contribute meaningfully to discussions within various communities. This approach not only helps you understand the community dynamics but also builds rapport with other members and establishes your credibility as a valuable participant.

3. Build Your Profile

Create a strong and professional profile that highlights your expertise in retail planning and technology. Use a clear profile picture, fill out your bio with relevant information, and include any certifications or credentials you have in the field. Creating a strong and professional profile is essential for establishing credibility and attracting opportunities in your field.

It is essential to have a few things in mind while creating a compelling profile:

Have a professional looking smart photo.

Keep your bio relevant with all your accomplishments, skills, interests, areas of expertise, and experience. Tailor your experience section to highlight the skills and expertise most relevant to your target audience. Remember to update regularly to reflect any changes in career or skills.

List your educational background, certifications or credentials. Tailor your experience section to highlight the skills and expertise most relevant to your target audience.

Create a separate section to showcase your skills and expertise. Include both technical skills (e.g., programming languages, software proficiency) and soft skills (e.g., communication, leadership).

Use endorsements from colleagues or supervisors to validate your skills and expertise. (Displaying endorsements and recommendations can enhance your credibility and trustworthiness.)

Engage and network actively with your connections by sharing relevant articles, participating in discussions, and congratulating others on their achievements. Join professional groups and communities related to your field to expand your network and stay updated on industry trends. Personalize connection requests by mentioning mutual interests or shared connections to increase the likelihood of acceptance.

Here's a detailed guide to help you build a compelling profile. Once your profile is created, remember to maintain an active presence on the platform to maximize your visibility and engagement with your network.

4. Provide Value

Start participating in discussions by offering valuable insights, sharing relevant articles or resources, and answering questions within your area of expertise. Focus on providing helpful and actionable advice that demonstrates your knowledge and experience. When participating in discussions and providing value, it's essential to focus on sharing insights, resources, and advice that are helpful and actionable. Here's a breakdown with some tips.

- **Know Your Audience:** Understand the people you're engaging with. Tailor your contributions to their level of expertise and interests.
- **Stay Informed:** Keep yourself updated with the latest trends, news, and research in your field. This allows you to offer relevant and timely information.
- **Listen First:** Before jumping in with your own thoughts, take the time to listen to what others are saying. This shows respect and helps you understand the context better.
- **Provide Insights:** Offer unique perspectives or insights that others may not have considered. This could be based on your experience, research, or observations.
- **Share Resources:** Whenever possible, share articles, studies, or resources that support your points. This adds credibility to your contributions and gives others additional material to explore.
- **Be Concise:** While it's important to provide valuable information, it's equally crucial to be concise. Respect others' time by getting to the point quickly and avoiding unnecessary fluff.
- **Ask Questions:** Don't hesitate to ask insightful questions that provoke further discussion or clarify points. This demonstrates your engagement and encourages others to share their thoughts.

- **Be Respectful:** Maintain a respectful tone, even if you disagree with someone. Constructive criticism is valuable, but it should always be delivered in a respectful manner.
- **Follow Up:** If someone asks for clarification or further information, be prompt in responding. This shows that you're engaged and willing to help others understand.
- **Stay Positive:** Keep a positive attitude throughout your interactions. Positivity encourages collaboration and fosters a supportive community environment.

By following these tips, you can effectively participate in discussions and provide value by offering insights, sharing resources, and engaging with others in a constructive manner.

5. Engage Authentically

Engage with other community members authentically by asking questions, responding to comments, and fostering meaningful conversations. Avoid overly promotional or self-serving behavior; instead, focus on building genuine connections with others in the community. Engaging authentically in a community involves actively participating in discussions, asking insightful questions, and contributing to meaningful conversations without solely promoting oneself or one's agenda. Here are some tips to help you engage authentically:

- **Listen, Understand, and Ask:** Take the time to listen to what others are saying before jumping into a conversation. Understand the context and perspectives shared by community members. Then, ask questions that demonstrate genuine interest and curiosity.

- **Provide Constructive Feedback:** When responding to comments or contributing to discussions, offer constructive feedback or insights that add value to the conversation. Avoid dismissive or overly critical remarks.
- **Share Personal Experiences:** Share your own experiences, stories, or insights relevant to the topic at hand. Authenticity often comes from personal anecdotes that others can relate to.
- **Be Respectful and Courteous:** Treat others with respect and kindness, even if you disagree with their opinions. Avoid hostile or confrontational language, and focus on fostering a positive and inclusive atmosphere.
- **Acknowledge Contributions:** Recognize and appreciate the contributions of others in the community. Respond to comments, express gratitude for valuable insights, and encourage further discussion.
- **Avoid Self-Promotion:** While it's okay to occasionally share relevant content or achievements, avoid constantly promoting yourself or your products/services. Focus on adding value to the community rather than solely promoting your own agenda.
- **Be Genuine and Transparent:** Authenticity shines through when you're genuine and transparent in your interactions. Avoid pretending to be someone you're not or using manipulative tactics to gain attention.
- **Engage Consistently:** Build relationships and trust within the community by engaging regularly. Consistent participation shows that you're committed to the community's goals and values.
- **Stay Open-Minded:** Be open to new ideas, perspectives, and feedback from others. Engaging authentically means being

willing to learn and grow from the diverse viewpoints present within the community.

By following these tips, you can engage authentically in community discussions, foster meaningful connections, and contribute positively to the overall atmosphere. Remember that authenticity is key to building trust and rapport with fellow community members.

6. Stay Active and Consistent

Consistency is key when it comes to building your presence in online communities. Make a commitment to regularly participate in discussions, share insights, and engage with other members over time. Here are some tips to help you stay active and consistent.

- **Set a Schedule:** Determine how often you want to engage with the community, whether it's daily, a few times a week, or weekly. Create a schedule and stick to it.
- **Quality over Quantity:** While consistency is important, ensure that your contributions are meaningful and add value to the community. Focus on quality interactions rather than just posting for the sake of posting.
- **Know Your Audience:** Understand the interests and preferences of the community members. Tailor your contributions to resonate with them and address their needs or concerns.
- **Engage with Others:** Actively participate in discussions, comment on other members' posts, and offer assistance or encouragement when needed. Building relationships with fellow members fosters a sense of community and encourages reciprocity.

- **Stay Informed:** Keep up to date with the latest trends, news, and discussions within the community's niche. Share relevant articles, resources, or updates to demonstrate your knowledge and expertise.
- **Use Multimedia:** Incorporate a variety of content formats such as text posts, images, videos, or infographics to keep your contributions engaging and diverse.
- **Respond Promptly:** Whenever someone engages with your posts or comments, make an effort to respond promptly. This shows that you're actively involved and value others' input.
- **Monitor Performance:** Keep track of how your contributions are received by the community. Pay attention to metrics such as likes, comments, and shares to gauge the impact of your engagement efforts.
- **Adjust and Iterate:** Continuously evaluate your approach and adapt based on feedback and performance data. Experiment with different types of content or engagement strategies to see what resonates best with the community.

By following these tips and making a consistent effort to engage with online communities, you can gradually build your presence, establish credibility, and foster meaningful connections with fellow members.

7. Demonstrate Thought Leadership

Position yourself as a thought leader in your domain by sharing original content, such as blog posts, case studies, or whitepapers, that showcases your expertise and insights on relevant topics. Establishing yourself as a thought leader in your domain requires a strategic approach to creating and sharing original content that demonstrates your expertise and insights on relevant topics. Here are some tips to help you effectively showcase your thought leadership.

- **Identify Your Niche:** Define the specific area within your domain where you have expertise and passion. Focus on topics that align with your strengths and interests, as this will help you create more impactful content.
- **Conduct Research:** Stay updated on industry trends, emerging technologies, and the latest developments in your field. Use reputable sources to gather information and insights that will help in your content creation process.
- **Create Valuable Content:** Develop high-quality content that provide unique perspectives, actionable advice, and solutions to common challenges within your domain. Use formats such as blog posts, case studies, whitepapers, infographics, videos, and podcasts.
- **Stay Authentic:** Share your personal experiences, anecdotes, and opinions to add authenticity to your content. People are more likely to resonate with your ideas if they perceive you as genuine and relatable.
- **Engage with Your Audience:** Encourage discussions and feedback by actively engaging with your audience on social media platforms, forums, and industry events. Respond to comments, answer questions, and participate in relevant conversations to build rapport and establish yourself as a trusted authority.
- **Collaborate with Others:** Partner with other thought leaders, influencers, and industry experts to co-create content,

participate in interviews, or collaborate on projects. Leveraging the collective expertise of your network can enhance your credibility and broaden your reach.

- **Leverage Multimedia Channels:** Experiment with different multimedia channels to amplify your message and reach a wider audience. Utilize platforms like LinkedIn, Medium, YouTube, and industry-specific forums to distribute your content and engage with diverse audiences.
- **Measure Your Impact:** Track key metrics such as website traffic, social media engagement, and audience feedback to evaluate the effectiveness of your thought leadership efforts. Use this data to refine your content strategy and optimize your approach over time.

By consistently producing valuable and insightful content, engaging with your audience, and staying abreast of industry trends, you can position yourself as a thought leader in your domain and establish credibility and influence within your professional community.

8. Network and Collaborate

Take advantage of networking opportunities within these communities to connect with other professionals, potential clients, or collaborators in the industry. Look for opportunities to collaborate on projects, share resources, or even organize events or webinars together. Networking and collaboration are essential components for professional growth and success in any industry. Here's a breakdown of how you can effectively utilize these strategies.

- **Identify Relevant Communities:** Join online forums, social media groups, professional associations, and industry-specific networks where professionals in your field gather. These could be platforms like LinkedIn groups, Reddit communities, or specialized forums related to your niche.
- **Engage and Contribute:** Once you've identified relevant communities, actively participate by sharing insights, commenting on discussions, and providing value to other members. Establish yourself as a knowledgeable and helpful contributor.
- **Build Relationships:** Networking is about building genuine relationships. Take the time to connect with other professionals by engaging in conversations, offering assistance, and showing interest in their work. Personalize your interactions and seek to understand their needs and interests.
- **Attend Events and Workshops:** Look for networking events, conferences, workshops, and seminars in your industry. These events provide valuable opportunities to meet new people, exchange ideas, and stay updated on industry trends. Don't hesitate to introduce yourself and strike up conversations with fellow attendees.
- **Utilize Online Platforms:** Leverage online platforms such as LinkedIn, Twitter, and professional networking sites to expand your network. Connect with professionals you admire or those

who work in complementary fields. Engage with their content, share relevant posts, and initiate conversations.

- **Seek Collaboration Opportunities:** Actively look for opportunities to collaborate with other professionals. This could involve teaming up on projects, sharing resources or expertise, co-authoring articles or research papers, or organizing joint events or webinars.
- **Be Proactive:** Don't wait for collaboration opportunities to come to you. Reach out to potential collaborators with clear and concise proposals outlining how you can mutually benefit from working together. Highlight your strengths, what you bring to the table, and how collaboration aligns with both parties' goals.
- **Follow Up and Maintain Relationships:** After making initial connections, follow up with your contacts to nurture the relationship. Keep in touch through periodic check-ins, sharing relevant updates or articles, or even arranging casual meetups. Building long-term relationships is key to sustained collaboration and networking success.
- **Be Generous and Supportive:** Offer help and support to your network whenever possible. Share relevant opportunities, provide recommendations or referrals, and celebrate the successes of your connections. Being a supportive member of your professional community can strengthen your relationships and reputation.

Remember to approach networking and collaboration with authenticity, respect, and a willingness to contribute to the success of others as well as your own.

9. Monitor and Evaluate

Continuously monitor the effectiveness of your participation in these communities by tracking metrics such as engagement levels, connections made, and opportunities generated. Use this data to adjust your approach and optimize your strategy over time. Monitoring and evaluating your participation in online communities is crucial to ensure that your efforts are effective and yielding desired outcomes. Here's a breakdown of how to do this effectively.

- **Define Metrics:** Start by defining specific metrics that align with your goals. These could include:
  - **Engagement levels:** Measure likes, comments, shares, and overall interaction with your posts or contributions.
  - **Connections made:** Track the number of new connections/followers you gain within the community.
  - **Opportunities generated:** Keep tabs on any business leads, collaborations, or opportunities that arise as a result of your participation.
- **Use Analytics Tools:** Leverage analytics tools provided by the platform itself or third-party tools to gather data on the defined metrics. For example, on social media platforms, you can use built-in analytics dashboards or tools like Google Analytics for tracking website traffic originating from the community.
- **Regular Monitoring:** Make it a habit to regularly monitor these metrics. Depending on the frequency of your activity and the platform's dynamics, this could be daily, weekly, or monthly.

- **Compare and Analyze:** Compare your performance over time and analyze any trends or patterns. Look for spikes or dips in engagement and try to understand what caused them. For instance, did certain types of content perform better than others? Did a particular topic resonate more with the community?
- **Seek Feedback:** Actively solicit feedback from community members to gauge their perception of your contributions. This can provide valuable insights into areas for improvement.
- **Adjust and Optimize:** Based on your analysis, adjust your approach accordingly. If you notice that certain types of content or engagement tactics are more effective, focus more on those. Similarly, if you're not seeing the desired results, experiment with different strategies until you find what works best.
- **Stay Flexible:** Communities evolve, as do your goals and priorities. Stay flexible and be willing to adapt your strategy as needed to stay aligned with changing dynamics.
- **Document Learnings:** Keep a record of your observations, learnings, and the actions you've taken based on them. This documentation can serve as a valuable reference for future iterations of your strategy.

By continuously monitoring and evaluating your participation in online communities, you'll be better equipped to optimize your approach and maximize the impact of your efforts over time.

10. Be Patient and Persistent

Building a presence and reputation in online communities takes time and effort, so be patient and persistent in your approach.

Consistently providing value and engaging with others will eventually lead to recognition and opportunities within the community. Building a presence and reputation in online communities requires dedication and a strategic approach. Here are some tips.

- **Be Patient**
  - Understand that building a reputation online takes time. It's not an overnight process.
  - Recognize that consistency and longevity are key factors in establishing credibility.
  - Don't get discouraged by slow progress or initial lack of recognition. Keep pushing forward.
- **Be Persistent**
  - Stay committed to your goals of building a presence and reputation within the community.
  - Consistently show up and engage with others on a regular basis.
  - Be persistent in adding value to discussions and offering assistance where you can.
- **Provide Value**
  - Focus on providing valuable contributions to the community. This could be through sharing knowledge, insights, resources, or even just offering support and encouragement.
  - Demonstrate your expertise in your niche by sharing helpful tips, tutorials, or case studies.

- Aim to solve problems and address the needs of other community members.

- **Engage Actively**
  - Actively participate in discussions by commenting, asking questions, and sharing your thoughts and experiences.
  - Be genuine and authentic in your interactions. People can often tell when someone is being insincere or overly promotional.
  - Take the time to listen to others and respond thoughtfully to their contributions.

- **Build Relationships**
  - Invest time in building genuine relationships with other members of the community. This can lead to mutual support and collaboration.
  - Acknowledge and appreciate the contributions of others. This fosters goodwill and strengthens your connections within the community.
  - Look for opportunities to connect with influencers or key figures in the community, but do so in a respectful and genuine manner.

- **Stay Consistent**
  - Consistency is key to maintaining momentum and building trust within the community.
  - Set aside dedicated time each day or week to engage with the community and create content.
  - Stick to your posting schedule and continue to show up even when results may not be immediately apparent.

LinkedIn is a great platform for online networking that I appreciate a lot, and it's a great platform to gain insights and build a supportive network. However, some networking tactics can be quite frustrating, and these blunders can make LinkedIn networking fail.

Here are some common blunders that I often see on LinkedIn:

- Immediate sales pitches upon first contact (Launching into a sales pitch faster than a squirrel on caffeine)
- Ignoring the personal element in networking (Treating networking like a one-way street, forgetting it takes two to LinkedIn tango)
- Constantly talking only about your own needs (Becoming the LinkedIn version of a broken record, endlessly singing your own tune)
- Repeated messages to non-responsive contacts (Persistently tapping the send button like it owes you money, despite the deafening silence)
- Pushing for a meeting too early in the relationship (Racing to schedule a meeting quicker than a contestant on "Speed Networking: LinkedIn Edition")
- Generic automated messages to every new connection (Spamming connections with automated messages like a bot stuck in an infinite loop)
- Not respecting the pace and preferences of the contact (Ignoring the fact that patience is a virtue, especially in the LinkedIn universe)

- Sending the same message to everyone, regardless of their interests (Copy-pasting messages with the precision of a scattergun, hoping something sticks like spaghetti on a wall)

Remember, LinkedIn is a virtual cocktail party, not a sales convention. Keep it light, keep it fun, and above all, keep it human!

By following these tips and maintaining a patient and persistent mindset, you can gradually build a strong presence and reputation within online communities. Remember that it's a journey, and success won't happen overnight. Stay focused on adding value, engaging with others, and building meaningful connections, and you'll eventually reap the rewards of your efforts.

6

REVOLUTIONIZING SALES—THE CURRENT LANDSCAPE AND FUTURE PROSPECTS OF AI

In the world of sales, where every interaction counts and every decision can sway the course of business fortunes, the integration of artificial intelligence (AI) has been nothing short of transformative. From automating routine tasks to providing invaluable insights, AI has become an indispensable tool for sales professionals in the modern era.

The traditional approach (relied heavily on manual processes: countless cold-calling, generic emails, etc.) was not only time-consuming but also inefficient, as it often resulted in low conversion rates and wasted resources. On the other hand, with the advent of AI in sales, these manual tasks have been revolutionized. AI-powered tools can now analyze vast amounts of data to identify high-quality leads more accurately and efficiently than ever before. For example, AI algorithms can analyze past customer interactions and behaviors to predict which leads are most likely to convert, allowing sales reps to prioritize their efforts accordingly. This not only saves time but also increases the likelihood of closing deals successfully.

Moreover, AI-driven CRM systems provide real-time insights into customer preferences and buying patterns, enabling sales professionals to personalize their approach and tailor their pitches accordingly. This level of customization was virtually impossible with conventional sales techniques, where sales reps often had to rely on guesswork or intuition.

However, it's essential to note that while AI has transformed the sales landscape, it's not a magic bullet. Human connection and rapport-building still play a crucial role in sales success. While AI can analyze data and streamline processes, it's ultimately up to the sales professional to build trust and nurture relationships with clients. So, while AI has certainly revolutionized sales by automating routine tasks and providing valuable insights, it's essential to strike a balance between technology and human touch to achieve optimal results. After all, even the most advanced AI algorithms can't replace the authenticity and empathy that human interaction brings to the sales process.

Having said that, the utilization of AI-powered customer relationship management (CRM) systems has become extremely efficient. These systems not only automate routine tasks like data entry and lead management but also provide invaluable insights into customer behaviors and preferences.

For example, imagine Sarah, a sales representative at a software company, who relies on an AI-driven CRM to manage her leads. With the help of AI, Sarah's CRM automatically sorts through incoming leads, prioritizing them based on their likelihood to convert. This frees up Sarah's time to focus on engaging with high-potential prospects rather than sifting through a mountain of leads manually.

Let's have a scenario. Dave, the ever-busy sales manager, recently started using an AI-powered assistant called Salesbot to automate his client follow-ups. Salesbot is designed to send personalized emails after each meeting, using transcriptions and sentiment analysis to craft just the right message. One day, after a particularly intense negotiation call with a tough client, Dave wraps up the meeting feeling unsure about how it went. Moments later, he checks his "Sent" folder ... and freezes. Salesbot had sent a follow-up email that read:

"Hi Jordan, it was interesting discussing your unique pricing strategy today. I'm sure your competitors would be fascinated by your approach!"

Salesbot, trying to be clever with sarcasm detection, interpreted Dave's dry tone during the call as witty enthusiasm. Dave now has to call the client back to clarify that he does respect their pricing—and no, he's not threatening to leak anything to the competitor. Lesson learned: AI is powerful, but context and nuance are still very human domains. Always double-check your AI-generated messages—especially when they could sound like passive-aggressive poetry.

In essence, AI in sales is a powerful ally, streamlining processes and providing valuable insights. But a touch of human oversight never hurts.

But AI's influence doesn't stop at customer interactions. Oh no, dear reader, it extends deep into sales forecasting and strategy. With access to vast troves of historical data, AI algorithms can analyze market trends, competitor behavior, and economic indicators with a level of nuance that would make even the most seasoned sales analyst blush (or perhaps green with envy). Armed with this insight, sales teams can make more informed decisions, anticipate market fluctuations, and adjust their strategies accordingly. It's like having a crystal ball that's been upgraded with a PhD in economics—minus the ominous music and swirling mist.

Of course, no discussion of AI in sales would be complete without mentioning the marvel that is predictive analytics. By crunching numbers and analyzing past performance, AI can forecast future sales trends with a degree of accuracy that borders on clairvoyance. Want to know which products are likely to fly off the shelves next quarter? AI's got you covered. Curious about which customers are most likely to return? AI can pinpoint them with the precision of a laser-guided missile—metaphorically speaking, of course. After all, we wouldn't want to give the impression that AI is plotting world domination. Or would we? Cue dramatic music.

Dear reader, the integration of AI into the sales process has indeed revolutionized the way businesses operate, ushering in an era of unprecedented efficiency, insight, and—dare I say—humor. So, the next time you find yourself marveling at the uncanny accuracy of a sales forecast or engaging in a spirited conversation with a chatbot, just remember, behind the curtain lies the tireless intellect of AI, tirelessly crunching numbers and—dare I say—occasionally cracking a joke. After all, even machines need a sense of humor. Allow me to guide you through a tour of some of the current applications of AI in sales as well as the exciting possibilities that lie ahead in the foreseeable future.

Current Applications

- **Lead Generation and Qualification:** AI-powered algorithms sift through vast troves of data to identify promising leads, saving time and effort for sales teams. By analyzing past interactions and customer behaviors, AI can predict which prospects are most likely to convert, enabling sales reps to focus their efforts where they're likely to yield the highest returns.

Ah, the marvels of AI in lead generation and qualification! Imagine a team of tireless digital scholars tirelessly sifting through the vast library of data, akin to diligent academics poring over dusty tomes in search of hidden insights. These AI-powered algorithms, armed with computational prowess rivaling the finest minds, embark on a quest to uncover the holy grail of prospects.

Consider this scenario: Picture me, the intrepid sales rep, armed with nothing but my wits and a trusty AI companion. Together, we venture forth into the labyrinth of data, where every click, scroll, and download serves as a breadcrumb guiding us toward potential leads. With the precision of a seasoned scholar, the AI dissects past interactions and deciphers the intricate dance of customer behaviors, much like a historian unraveling the mysteries of ancient civilizations.

Ahem. Picture the AI as a professor emeritus, adorned in digital tweed, stroking its metaphorical beard as it pontificates on the probabilities of conversion. "Ah, yes," it murmurs in its algorithmic lilt, "based on the patterns observed in the annals of data, this prospect exhibits a propensity for purchase comparable to that of a student gravitating toward extra credit."

Armed with these insights, I, the humble sales rep, can focus my efforts with laser-like precision, targeting those prospects deemed most likely to yield a fruitful conversion. It's akin to conducting a scholarly debate, where each engagement is a thesis defended and every conversion a triumphant conclusion worthy of publication. In essence, AI in lead generation and qualification is the academic pursuit of sales excellence, where data becomes the canvas upon which we paint our sales strategies, and each prospect a potential citation in the grand bibliography of success.

- **Personalized Sales Outreach:** With AI-driven personalization, sales pitches can be tailored to resonate with individual prospects on a deeper level. Natural Language Processing (NLP) algorithms analyze communication patterns and preferences, allowing sales reps to craft messages that strike the right chord and drive engagement.

The art of personalized sales outreach—where AI-driven wizardry meets the finesse of human communication! Here you are, armed with the power of NLP algorithms at your fingertips, and these clever bits of code analyze communication patterns with the finesse of a linguistic detective, uncovering the hidden preferences and nuances of your prospects.

Imagine your NLP algorithm as the diligent student poring over a centuries-old manuscript, deciphering the cryptic codes of Chaucer or Shakespeare. Only instead of deciphering sonnets, it's unraveling email threads and social media interactions. Now, armed with this insight, you, the sales virtuoso, can craft pitches that resonate on a level so deep, it's like you're whispering sweet nothings directly into your prospect's ear. You know their pain points, their desires, their favorite memes—okay, maybe not the memes, but you get the idea.

Here's a whimsical example: Let's say your prospect is a CEO who fancies themselves a connoisseur of fine coffee. Your NLP algorithm reveals this penchant for caffeine excellence, so instead of a generic pitch, you craft a message likening your product to the perfect espresso—bold, refined, and guaranteed to kick-start their day (and their business) with gusto.

With AI-driven personalization, your sales pitch isn't just another email cluttering up their inbox; it's a tailored experience, a bespoke suit in a world of off-the-rack solutions. And as any scholar will tell you, there's nothing quite like the satisfaction of a perfectly crafted argument—or sales pitch—hitting its mark with precision.

Sales Forecasting: Leveraging historical data and predictive analytics, AI empowers organizations to forecast sales with unprecedented accuracy. By identifying patterns and trends, businesses can anticipate market fluctuations, adjust their strategies accordingly, and make informed decisions about resource allocation and inventory management.

Imagine you're the proud owner of an artisanal bookstore. Your quaint shop nestled in a bustling neighborhood has been thriving for years, but you're always looking for ways to improve your business acumen. Here's how AI and predictive analytics can revolutionize your sales forecasting:

a) **Historical Data Analysis:** Delving into the store's transaction records, AI swiftly sifts through years of sales data. Patterns emerge, such as seasonal trends and unexpected fluctuations like a surge in demand for classic literature during the colder months, perhaps driven by local reading groups.

b) **Predictive Modeling:** Equipped with advanced algorithms, predictive models are constructed to anticipate future sales with remarkable accuracy. These models factor in various variables like upcoming events, holidays, and even weather forecasts, as rainy days often correlate with increased book purchases (because, let's face it, nothing beats curling up with a good book on a rainy day).

c) **Market Fluctuations and Strategy Adjustments:** With predictive analytics you can adeptly navigate market shifts. If the data suggests a decline in demand for a particular genre, such as romance novels, you can adjust your inventory accordingly, ensuring shelves are stocked with titles aligned with current trends.

d) **Resource Allocation and Inventory Management:** With great forecasting power comes great responsibility ... to manage your inventory wisely! No more overstocked shelves groaning under the weight of neglected tomes or frantic last-minute orders to replenish bestselling titles. AI helps us strike the perfect balance, ensuring that every square inch of shelf space is optimized for maximum profitability.

So, leveraging historical data and predictive analytics through AI can indeed empower businesses to forecast sales with unprecedented accuracy, navigate market fluctuations with aplomb, and emerge victorious in the ever-epic battle for bookstore supremacy.

- **Customer Relationship Management (CRM):** AI-driven CRM platforms serve as centralized hubs for customer data, enabling sales teams to gain deep insights into customer behavior and preferences. By leveraging machine learning, these systems can identify patterns and recommend personalized upselling and cross-selling opportunities, ultimately increasing customer lifetime value.

For example, a company like Scholarly Solutions Inc., which provides academic writing tools to researchers, can use an AI-powered CRM to track user interactions, such as website visits or webinar attendance. If a long-time customer frequently explores features related to citation management, the system can automatically flag this interest and suggest tailored product bundles. It can even automate personalized outreach based on the customer's research focus and past behavior, making engagement both timely and relevant.

In short, AI-driven CRMs don't just manage customer data, they transform it into actionable insights, allowing businesses to build stronger, smarter, and more personalized relationships.

- **Sales Performance Optimization:** AI-powered analytics tools evaluate the performance of sales reps, identifying strengths and weaknesses and offering personalized coaching recommendations. By analyzing factors such as call duration, conversion rates, and closing techniques, these tools enable sales managers to optimize their teams' performance and drive better outcomes.

Imagine a sales team at a fictional company, AcademiaTech—that specializes in selling educational software to universities, is looking to boost its sales performance. Leading the charge is Dr. Ivy League, the sales manager. With a diverse team of sales representatives—each bringing different strengths and facing unique challenges—Dr. Ivy League finds it difficult to identify who needs what kind of coaching to improve overall team effectiveness.

To address this, Dr. Ivy League implements an AI-powered analytics tool designed to evaluate sales performance in detail. This tool analyzes data from sales calls—such as call duration, conversion rates, and closing techniques—and generates personalized coaching insights for each team member.

Let's consider two members of the team:

Professor Persuader is known for his engaging and charismatic conversations with clients. However, the AI tool reveals that he often struggles with closing deals efficiently. It suggests coaching strategies focused on streamlining his closing techniques without losing his conversational charm.

Dr. Data-Driven, in contrast, provides thorough and informative product explanations but has difficulty establishing a personal connection with potential clients. The AI recommends techniques to help him build rapport and infuse more personality into his calls while still leveraging his strength in data-driven communication.

With these insights, Dr. Ivy League can tailor coaching plans to each sales rep's needs, rather than relying on one-size-fits-all training. The result: improved individual performance and a more effective sales team.

In a humorous twist, imagine the AI presenting its findings in a scholarly manner:

"Dear esteemed Dr. Ivy League, it appears that Professor Persuader's discourse possesses an eloquence that enthralls potential clients, akin to the captivating prose of Shakespeare. However, a gentle nudge toward expedited closure could transform these soliloquies into successful sales denouements."

"And for the erudite Dr. Data-Driven, while the exposition of product details rivals the precision of a peer-reviewed journal article, a dash of humor or personal anecdote may establish a more profound connection with clients, fostering camaraderie akin to that found in a colloquium."

Armed with these insights, Dr. Ivy League can provide targeted coaching recommendations tailored to each sales rep's unique style and areas for improvement. Whether it's refining closing techniques or enhancing rapport-building skills, the goal is to optimize the team's performance and drive better outcomes. In the end, with AI-powered analytics as their scholarly sidekick, AcademiaTech's sales team embarks on a journey of continuous improvement, blending the art of persuasion with the science of data-driven decision-making to achieve academic excellence in sales.

The Foreseeable Future

Looking ahead, the future of AI in sales holds even greater promise, with advancements in technology poised to further revolutionize the industry. Imagine a world where sales teams are empowered by AI algorithms that not only predict customer behavior but also tailor their approach in real time to maximize conversions. It's like having a personal assistant who knows exactly what each customer needs before they even realize it themselves. Picture an AI algorithm sitting in on a sales call, analyzing tonal nuances and micro-expressions with the precision of a seasoned psychologist. It's as if Freud himself has been reincarnated as a digital assistant, deciphering the subconscious desires of prospects with unparalleled accuracy.

But it doesn't stop there. With advancements in natural language processing, AI can sift through mountains of data to uncover hidden patterns and insights, guiding sales teams toward the most promising leads like a scholarly detective unraveling a complex mystery. Now, let's explore some of the advancements poised to revolutionize the industry:

- **Augmented Intelligence:** As AI continues to evolve, we're likely to see a shift toward augmented intelligence, where AI systems work in tandem with human sales professionals to enhance their capabilities. Rather than replacing humans, AI will empower them by providing real-time insights, automating repetitive tasks, and enabling more personalized interactions with customers.

Picture this: You're a sales professional navigating the labyrinthine world of client interactions, armed with your charm, wit, and a trusty AI sidekick. Let's call it ... SalesBot 9000.

As you engage in your daily dance of deals, SalesBot 9000 is tirelessly crunching numbers, analyzing market trends, and sifting through oceans of data faster than you can say "commission." Meanwhile, you're dazzling clients with your finely honed interpersonal skills, effortlessly weaving insights provided by SalesBot 9000 into your conversations like a maestro conducting a concerto.

In one instance, you find yourself in a tête-à-tête with a particularly persnickety client who demands statistical evidence to support your claims. Fear not, for SalesBot 9000 swoops in with an arsenal of peer-reviewed studies and industry reports, delivered with a dash of academic panache that would make even the most discerning scholar nod in approval.

Together, you and SalesBot 9000 navigate the treacherous waters of negotiation, seamlessly blending human intuition with AI precision. With each interaction, you're not just making sales, you're conducting a symphony of augmented intelligence, where the sum is greater than its parts.

And as the credits roll on another successful deal, you can't help but chuckle at the thought of SalesBot 9000 attending its own graduation ceremony from AI University, cap and gown adorned with lines of code. After all, in this brave new world of augmented intelligence, even machines deserve a little humor!

- **Predictive Analytics (Anticipating Tomorrow's Market, Today): As** data sources multiply and AI algorithms mature, predictive analytics is becoming a powerful force in reshaping how businesses understand and respond to market dynamics. By analyzing patterns in customer behavior, purchase history, online interactions, and even real-time sentiment, businesses can now anticipate needs with remarkable accuracy—turning raw data into strategic foresight.

Imagine a company like Eureka Electronics, a smart home device retailer. By leveraging predictive analytics, Eureka can analyze historical sales data, web browsing behavior, and regional weather trends. The result? Their sales team receives timely, data-driven insights—such as a forecasted spike in demand for smart thermostats before an approaching cold front. With this knowledge, they adjust inventory, launch targeted campaigns, and offer discounts to the right customers at exactly the right time.

This shift—from reactive to proactive selling—not only improves customer satisfaction but also drives profitability. Predictive analytics acts like a digital crystal ball, allowing teams to engage customers just before their intent peaks.

Even in academic circles, this field is gaining momentum. At a fictional conference titled *Predictive Analytics: Unraveling Market Mysteries*, experts humorously debate Bayesian inference versus machine learning. As Dr. Ivory Tower remarks, "It's like predicting a coin toss—only with more variables and fewer arguments about which side is heads." His colleague, Professor Data Crunch, adds, "It's solving a Rubik's Cube blindfolded … but with machine vision." In business and academia alike, the message is clear: predictive analytics transforms uncertainty into opportunity. For forward-thinking companies, it's not just about knowing what customers want—it's about knowing when they'll want it.

- **Hyper-Personalization:** AI-driven personalization will reach new heights, enabling sales reps to deliver hyper-personalized experiences tailored to the unique preferences and needs of individual customers. By leveraging advanced analytics and predictive modeling, businesses will be able to anticipate customer requirements at every stage of the sales journey, fostering deeper connections and driving customer loyalty. By leveraging machine learning algorithms, sales platforms can offer personalized product recommendations based on a customer's past purchases, preferences, and browsing history. It's akin to having a personal shopper who knows your tastes better than you do yourself.

Ah, the marvels of hyper-personalization in the realm of sales, where AI becomes the savoir-faire of every savvy sales representative! Picture this: A customer named Bob walks into a virtual storefront. Little does he know that the digital gears are already whirring behind the scenes, analyzing his past purchases, browsing history, and even his astrological sign (because why not?). Our trusty AI algorithms, let's call them "SalesBot 9000," have been meticulously trained on a diet of data and witty banter. As Bob peruses the digital shelves, SalesBot 9000 springs into action, crafting a personalized journey tailored to Bob's every whim and fancy. Drawing on Bob's penchant for vintage vinyl records, his recent interest in DIY home improvement, and his inexplicable obsession with miniature cacti, SalesBot 9000 deftly serves up recommendations that would make even the most seasoned salesperson nod in approval.

"Ah, Bob," chirps SalesBot 9000 in its virtual monotone, "I see you're a connoisseur of all things retro. Might I interest you in our limited edition, autographed Elvis Presley vinyl collection? It pairs quite nicely with your eclectic taste in home decor." Bob's eyes widen in surprise as he clicks on the offer, marveling at the uncanny accuracy of SalesBot 9000's recommendations. Little does he know, behind the scenes, SalesBot 9000 is chuckling to itself, patting its metaphorical back for a job well done.

And thus, the wonders of hyper-personalization continue to dazzle and delight—one personalized sales pitch at a time.

- **Conversational AI:** Natural Language Processing (NLP) technology will continue to advance, enabling the development of more sophisticated conversational AI interfaces. Virtual sales assistants powered by AI will engage with customers in natural, human-like conversations, providing instant support, answering queries, and guiding them through the sales process with ease. AI-powered chatbots and Virtual Assistants are becoming increasingly sophisticated, capable of handling customer inquiries, scheduling appointments, and even closing deals autonomously. It's like having a tireless assistant who never sleeps, ready to engage with customers 24/7.

Imagine you're a customer browsing an online store for a new pair of shoes. As you're perusing the options, a pop-up chat window appears, introducing itself as ShoeBot. You decide to engage with it, curious about how well it can assist you.

You: "Hello, ShoeBot! I'm looking for a pair of running shoes, but I'm not sure which brand would suit me best. Can you help?"

ShoeBot: "Greetings! I'd be delighted to assist you in your quest for the perfect running shoes. May I inquire about your usual running terrain and any specific preferences you have in mind?"

You: "Well, I mainly run on pavements, and I prefer shoes with good arch support. Oh, and a splash of color wouldn't hurt!"

ShoeBot: "Excellent choice! For pavement running with focus on arch support and a touch of style, may I suggest the 'SpeedRunner 9000'? It boasts superior arch support technology and comes in a variety of vibrant colors to match your personality."

You: "Hmm, sounds intriguing! But I'm still hesitant. Can you provide some customer reviews or perhaps compare it with another popular brand?"

ShoeBot: "Absolutely! Let me gather that information for you. While I do, here's a joke for you: Why did the shoe go to therapy? Because it had too many sole-searching issues!"

You chuckle at ShoeBot's attempt at humor as it swiftly retrieves the comparative data and customer reviews.

ShoeBot: "Based on the gathered data, the 'SpeedRunner 9000' has received rave reviews for its durability and comfort compared to its competitors. Would you like to proceed with this selection?"

You: "You know what, ShoeBot? I think you've convinced me! Let's go ahead and make the purchase."

ShoeBot: "Splendid! I'll handle the transaction seamlessly for you. Congratulations on your new shoes, and thank you for choosing ShoeBot's assistance. If you have any further inquiries or need assistance in the future, don't hesitate to reach out. I'm here 24/7 to serve you!"

In this scenario, ShoeBot exemplifies the advancements in conversational AI technology, seamlessly guiding the customer through the sales process with natural language interactions. Additionally, ShoeBot's integration of humor adds a touch of levity to the conversation, enhancing the overall customer experience.

As ShoeBot navigates the intricate maze of customer queries and product recommendations, it metaphorically treads upon the terra firma of linguistic algorithms, effortlessly balancing the scales of data retrieval and comedic relief. Much like a well-versed scholar, ShoeBot exhibits a mastery of both information dissemination and interpersonal engagement, epitomizing the pinnacle of conversational AI sophistication.

This blend of technological prowess and whimsical banter not only showcases the capabilities of AI-powered virtual assistants but also highlights the potential for enhancing customer interactions in ways previously unimaginable.

- **Sales Process Optimization:** Through the analysis of historical sales data, AI can identify inefficiencies in the sales process and suggest optimizations to improve performance. It's like having a sales coach who provides actionable insights based on empirical evidence rather than mere intuition.

Imagine a fictional company, Acme Widgets Inc., which specializes in selling widgets to various industries. They have a robust sales team but have noticed a stagnation in their sales growth. To address this, they decide to employ AI-driven sales process optimization.

Enter Professor Widgetstein, renowned in the field of Salesology (the science of sales). Professor Widgetstein has developed an AI algorithm called SalesGenius 9000. This algorithm analyzes vast amounts of historical sales data, including customer interactions, conversion rates, and sales pipeline velocity. Now, let's introduce our protagonist, Salesman Sam. Sam is a seasoned sales professional at Acme Widgets Inc. who has been struggling to meet his sales targets lately. He's eager to see how SalesGenius 9000 can help him improve his performance. As Salesman Sam eagerly awaits the results, SalesGenius 9000 starts crunching the numbers. It identifies several key inefficiencies in the sales process:

a) **Prospecting Pitfalls:** SalesGenius 9000 notices that Sam spends too much time chasing leads that are unlikely to convert. It suggests implementing a lead scoring system to prioritize high-quality leads based on past conversion data and customer profiles.
b) **Communication Conundrums:** The algorithm detects a pattern of delayed follow-ups and missed communication opportunities. It recommends automating follow-up emails and scheduling reminders to ensure timely interactions with prospects.
c) **Product Presentation Predicaments:** SalesGenius 9000 notices that Sam tends to use a one-size-fits-all approach during product presentations. It suggests tailoring presentations to each prospect's specific needs and pain points, utilizing personalized content and case studies.

d) **Closing Dilemmas:** Finally, the algorithm identifies that Sam struggles with overcoming objections and closing deals. It suggests providing him with objection handling scripts and negotiation tactics based on successful past interactions.

As Salesman Sam receives these recommendations, he can't help but chuckle at the thought of having an AI sales coach. "Looks like Professor Widgetstein's SalesGenius 9000 is here to save the day!" he quips. Armed with these actionable insights, Salesman Sam begins implementing the suggested optimizations. Over time, he starts to see a noticeable improvement in his sales performance. Thanks to the power of AI-driven sales process optimization, Acme Widgets Inc. experiences a resurgence in sales growth, much to the delight of Salesman Sam and his colleagues.

And thus, another success story is written in the annals of Salesology, where empirical evidence triumphs over mere intuition, and AI algorithms reign supreme in the quest for sales excellence.

Remember, when data meets humor, it's not just entertaining—it's statistically significant!

- **Ethical Considerations:** As AI becomes increasingly integrated into the sales ecosystem, ethical considerations surrounding data privacy, bias mitigation, and transparency will come to the forefront. Businesses will need to ensure that AI algorithms are trained on diverse and representative datasets, and that ethical guidelines are adhered to throughout the sales process to maintain trust and credibility with customers. Given below are some of the aspects of ethical consideration.

a) **Data Privacy:** Imagine a company implementing AI algorithms to analyze customer purchasing patterns. Without proper safeguards, this data could be misused, compromising customer privacy. For instance, if the AI system inadvertently starts correlating certain purchasing behaviors with sensitive personal information, such as medical conditions, it could lead to privacy breaches. To prevent this, robust data anonymization techniques must be employed. As an academic joke goes, "Even algorithms need to learn the art of discretion; they shouldn't spill the beans on what's in your shopping cart!"

b) **Bias Mitigation:** Consider an AI-powered sales recommendation system that inadvertently favors certain demographics over others. If the training data predominantly consists of purchases from a specific demographic group, the AI might inadvertently recommend products tailored to that group more often, perpetuating bias. To mitigate this, businesses must ensure their datasets are diverse and representative. As an academic quip would have it, "AI algorithms need a crash course in diversity, or they'll keep recommending bow ties to penguins!"

c) **Transparency:** Transparency is essential for maintaining trust. Customers should understand how AI algorithms influence sales decisions. For example, if a customer receives personalized product recommendations, they should know that these suggestions are driven by AI analysis of their past purchases and preferences. As an academic jest goes, "AI algorithms should be as transparent as a freshly cleaned lab beaker—no hidden ingredients, please!"

In conclusion, the modern-day use of AI in sales has already brought about significant improvements in efficiency, effectiveness, and customer engagement. Looking ahead, the future of AI in sales is brimming with potential, promising even greater levels of personalization, predictive insights, and augmented intelligence. By embracing these advancements responsibly and ethically, businesses can unlock new opportunities for growth and success in the ever-evolving landscape of sales.

Integrating AI into sales processes brings both opportunities and ethical challenges. Businesses must navigate these challenges with care, ensuring data privacy, bias mitigation, and transparency are prioritized. The future of AI in sales holds immense promise, with advancements poised to transform the industry in ways that were once only imaginable in the realms of science fiction. So, buckle up and get ready for a sales revolution powered by algorithms and data, and make complex concepts more approachable.

7

SETTING SAIL IN THE GLOBAL SALES SEAS

Ahoy there, fellow sales navigators! Welcome aboard as we embark on a journey through the tumultuous yet exhilarating waters of global B2B sales. As a global sales head, I've weathered many storms, danced with countless clients across continents, and learned a thing or two about the art and science of sealing deals on a worldwide scale.

Embracing the Chaos: A Tale of Global Ventures

Picture this: jet lag, time zones, cultural nuances, and language barriers—the typical buffet of challenges awaiting any global sales leader. But fear not, for where there's chaos, there's also opportunity.

I recall one particularly memorable trip to China, where I found myself bowing more times than I could count and navigating a maze of business card exchanges. But amidst the confusion, I discovered the power of respect for local customs and the importance of building relationships beyond borders. Remember, in global sales, it's not just about what you're selling; it's about who you're selling it to.

Crafting the Global Sales Arsenal

In the battlefield of global sales, one must arm themselves with an arsenal of techniques tailored to each market's unique landscape. Here are a few tried-and-tested tactics from my own playbook:

Cultural Intelligence

Understanding cultural nuances isn't just a nice-to-have; it's a must-have. Whether you're sealing deals in Shanghai or striking agreements in São Paulo, taking the time to understand cultural sensitivities can be the difference between a handshake and a closed door.

Let's explore the concept of cultural intelligence (CQ) with an example involving business negotiations between a western company and a Japanese corporation. Imagine a scenario where a US-based technology firm is seeking to establish a partnership with a Japanese electronics manufacturer to develop and market a new line of smartphones. The American team, well-versed in their product's technical specifications and market potential, travels to Tokyo for the negotiations.

In this scenario, cultural intelligence plays a crucial role in determining the success of the negotiations. Here's how:

- **Understanding Communication Styles:** Japanese business culture often emphasizes indirect communication and consensus-building. Unlike the assertive and direct communication style commonly found in the United States, the Japanese tend to prioritize harmony and group cohesion. Therefore, the American team needs to adapt their communication style to be more subtle, respectful, and attentive to non-verbal cues during the negotiations.
- **Respecting Hierarchy and Protocol:** In Japanese culture, respect for hierarchy and seniority is paramount. Decision-making processes can be slow, as consensus is typically

reached through careful consideration and consultation with senior members. The American team must be patient and demonstrate respect for the hierarchical structure within the Japanese company, ensuring they address the most senior members first and defer to their authority.

- **Building Trust through Relationship Building:** Japanese business relationships are often built on trust and long-term commitment. Before diving into the specifics of the partnership, the American team should invest time in building rapport and establishing personal connections with their Japanese counterparts. This might involve socializing outside of formal meetings, exchanging gifts, and demonstrating genuine interest in the Japanese culture and values.
- **Navigating Decision-Making Processes:** In Japan, decisions are typically made collectively, with input from various stakeholders. While the American team might be accustomed to making quick decisions based on individual authority, they need to adapt to the Japanese consensus-driven approach. This requires patience and an understanding that negotiations may progress slowly as consensus is reached among all parties involved.

By demonstrating cultural intelligence in these areas, the American team can enhance their chances of success in negotiating a partnership with the Japanese electronics manufacturer. Failure to understand and respect the cultural nuances could lead to misunderstandings, frustration, and ultimately, a breakdown in negotiations. Therefore, cultural intelligence isn't just a nice-to-have; it's essential for bridging cultural gaps and fostering productive international business relationships.

Adaptability

Flexibility is the name of the game in global sales. Embrace change, pivot when necessary, and always be ready to adjust your strategy on the fly. Remember, the only constant in global sales is unpredictability. In global sales, adaptability and flexibility are essential traits for success due to the ever-changing nature of the market.

- **Embrace Change:** Imagine you're a global sales manager for a technology company offering cybersecurity solutions. With the rise of remote work due to the COVID-19 pandemic, there's been a surge in demand for secure virtual private network (VPN) services. Embracing this change, your sales team pivots from traditional B2B sales to also targeting individual consumers who are now working from home. By adapting your sales approach to meet the evolving needs of the market, you capitalize on the increased demand for cybersecurity solutions in the remote work era.
- **Pivot When Necessary:** Suppose that you're a sales director for a fashion brand expanding into international markets. Just as you're about to launch a major advertising campaign highlighting your spring collection, a global supply chain disruption leads to delays in product shipments. Instead of sticking to your original plan, you quickly pivot by leveraging social media to engage with customers, offering exclusive pre-order discounts and virtual styling sessions. By adapting

your strategy in response to the supply chain challenge, you maintain customer engagement and minimize the impact on sales.

- **Adjust Strategy on the Fly:** Consider you're a sales executive for a pharmaceutical company launching a new drug in a competitive market. After initial sales projections fall short due to regulatory hurdles in certain regions, you adjust your strategy on the fly by focusing on fast-track approvals in markets with less stringent regulations. Additionally, you reallocate resources to ramp up educational campaigns targeting healthcare providers in regions where the drug has received approval. By agilely adjusting your strategy based on market feedback and regulatory dynamics, you accelerate market penetration and drive sales growth.
- **The Only Constant is Unpredictability:** Let's say you're a sales manager for a global automotive manufacturer facing uncertainty due to fluctuating tariffs and trade tensions between key markets. Rather than trying to predict the outcome of trade negotiations, you build flexibility into your supply chain by diversifying sourcing options and establishing strategic partnerships with local suppliers in multiple regions. This enables your company to adapt quickly to changing trade dynamics and minimize disruptions in production and sales. By accepting the unpredictability of the global trade landscape, you mitigate risks and maintain a competitive edge in the market.

By staying agile and responsive to market dynamics, sales professionals can navigate challenges and capitalize on opportunities in an ever-evolving global marketplace.

Local Partnerships

When in Rome, do as the Romans do; or better yet, partner with them. Collaborating with local experts can provide invaluable insights and pave the way for smoother sailing in unfamiliar waters. Collaborating with local partners can be extremely beneficial when entering a new market or navigating unfamiliar territory. Let me try to illustrate this concept with a few examples.

- **Cultural Understanding:** When Airbnb expanded into China, they faced unique challenges due to cultural differences and regulatory complexities. To tackle this, they partnered with local companies like Alibaba and invested in understanding the preferences and behaviors of Chinese travelers. This approach allowed Airbnb to tailor its services to the local market, leading to significant growth in China.
- **Navigating Legal and Regulatory Landscape:** Uber's entry into various international markets has been met with regulatory hurdles and opposition. In India, for instance, Uber faced resistance from local taxi unions and regulatory agencies. However, through partnerships with local legal experts and government officials, Uber was able to address regulatory concerns and adapt its business model to comply with local laws, enabling its expansion across the country.
- **Access to Distribution Channels:** When Starbucks entered Japan, it formed a partnership with Sazaby League, a local

retail company with expertise in the Japanese market. This partnership allowed Starbucks to leverage Sazaby's extensive network of retail locations and distribution channels, facilitating rapid expansion and establishing a strong presence in Japan.

- **Market Insights and Customer Preferences:** Walmart's acquisition of a majority stake in Flipkart, India's leading e-commerce platform, provided Walmart with valuable insights into the preferences and shopping habits of Indian consumers. By partnering with a local player, Walmart gained access to data and analytics that helped them tailor their product offerings and marketing strategies to better suit the needs of Indian customers.
- **Overcoming Language and Cultural Barriers:** When Netflix expanded its streaming service to countries with diverse linguistic and cultural backgrounds, such as Spain and Japan, it collaborated with local content creators and production companies to develop original content that resonated with local audiences. By partnering with local talent, Netflix was able to overcome language barriers and cultural differences, thereby increasing its appeal and subscriber base in these markets.

In each of these examples, collaborating with local partners provided companies with valuable insights, resources, and expertise that helped them navigate unfamiliar territories and establish a strong presence in new markets.

Technology as a Bridge

In today's interconnected world, technology serves as our trusty bridge across continents. From virtual meetings to CRM systems, leverage technology to shrink the globe and take you closer to your clients. Here are some examples to illustrate this.

- **Virtual Meetings and Teleconferencing:** Platforms like Zoom, Microsoft Teams, and Skype have revolutionized how businesses communicate globally. Teams from different corners of the world can now meet face-to-face virtually, discussing projects, negotiating deals, and building relationships in real time. This not only saves time and resources but also fosters collaboration on a global scale.
- **Customer Relationship Management (CRM) Systems:** CRM systems such as Salesforce, HubSpot, and Zoho provide a centralized database for storing customer information, tracking interactions, and analyzing data to personalize communication and improve customer satisfaction.
- **E-commerce Platforms:** Online marketplaces like Amazon, Alibaba, and eBay connect buyers and sellers from around the world, facilitating cross-border trade. Through e-commerce platforms, businesses can reach a global audience, sell their products or services internationally, and streamline the purchasing process for customers regardless of their location.
- **Remote Work Tools:** With the rise of remote work, tools like Slack, Asana, and Trello have become essential for teams to collaborate efficiently irrespective of their physical location. These platforms enable real-time communication, task

management, and project tracking, ensuring remote teams stay connected and productive.

- **Language Translation Services:** Language barriers can often hinder global communication, but technology has bridged this gap with services like Google Translate and Microsoft Translator. These tools provide instant translation of text, speech, and even images, facilitating smooth communication between individuals who speak different languages.
- **Blockchain Technology:** Blockchain technology has the potential to revolutionize international transactions and supply chain management by providing secure, transparent, and efficient systems for recording and verifying transactions. Platforms like IBM Blockchain and Ethereum are already being used to streamline cross-border payments, track the provenance of goods, and ensure the authenticity of products.
- **Social Media Platforms:** Social media platforms such as Facebook, Instagram, and LinkedIn allow businesses to connect with a global audience, build brand awareness, and engage with customers across borders. Through targeted advertising and content marketing, businesses can reach potential clients worldwide and cultivate meaningful relationships with them.

By leveraging these technologies and more, businesses can effectively shrink the globe, overcome geographical barriers, and bring themselves closer to their clients and partners around the world.

Navigating the Leadership Compass

Leading a global sales team isn't for the faint hearted, but with the right compass in hand, you can chart a course to success. Here are a few tips to keep in mind.

Lead by Example

As a global sales leader, your team takes cues from you. Demonstrate resilience, adaptability, and a relentless pursuit of excellence in everything you do. Leading by example is crucial for any leader, especially in a global sales environment where teams look to their leader for guidance, inspiration, and motivation.

- **Resilience:** Resilience is about bouncing back from setbacks and challenges. As a sales leader, you might face rejection, market downturns, or product challenges. Your response to these situations sets the tone for your team. For example: If a major client unexpectedly pulls out of a deal, instead of dwelling on the loss, you can immediately start strategizing with your team on how to fill the gap. Share personal anecdotes of times when you faced setbacks but ultimately succeeded. This humanizes you as a leader and shows that setbacks are just temporary roadblocks.
- **Adaptability:** Your ability to pivot strategies, embrace new technologies, and adjust to market dynamics will inspire your team to do the same. Consider introducing new sales tools or techniques and leading by example by mastering them first. This could be adopting a new CRM system, leveraging social selling platforms, or implementing data analytics for better decision-making. Encourage your team to explore emerging

markets or product lines. Show them that you're willing to step out of your comfort zone and learn alongside them.

- **Relentless pursuit of excellence:** Striving for excellence means constantly pushing the boundaries of what's possible and never settling for mediocrity. Here's how you can demonstrate this. Set high standards for yourself and your team and hold everyone accountable for meeting them. Celebrate successes but also analyze failures to learn and improve. Lead by example in continuous learning and development. Attend workshops, seminars, and industry conferences, and encourage your team to do the same. Share insights and best practices from these events with your team. Recognize and reward exceptional performance. Publicly acknowledge team members who consistently go above and beyond and highlight their achievements as examples for others to emulate.

By embodying these qualities and behaviors, you not only inspire your team to perform at their best but also create a culture of resilience, adaptability, and excellence within your sales organization.

Communicate, Communicate, Communicate

Effective communication is the lifeblood of global sales. Keep the lines open, foster transparency, and ensure that every member of your team is on the same page. Effective communication is indeed vital in global sales, as it ensures alignment, transparency, and efficiency within a team. Let's break down each aspect and explore with some examples.

- **Keeping the Lines Open:** In global sales, teams often operate across different time zones and cultural backgrounds. Keeping communication channels open ensures that team members can reach out for clarification, updates, or support whenever needed. For instance, a sales team based in the United States might need to collaborate with a development team in India. By utilizing tools like Slack, Zoom, or even asynchronous communication methods like email, they can maintain constant communication despite the time difference.
- **Fostering Transparency:** Transparency builds trust within a team and with clients. When everyone is aware of the progress, challenges, and goals, they can work together more effectively. Consider a scenario where a sales team is negotiating a deal with a client. Transparent communication about pricing, timelines, and potential obstacles helps in managing expectations and preventing misunderstandings. This transparency can be facilitated through regular status updates, progress reports, and honest discussions about challenges and setbacks.
- **Ensuring Alignment:** In global sales, alignment is crucial to ensure that every member of the team understands the overall strategy and their role within it. Without alignment, efforts may become disjointed, leading to missed opportunities or conflicting actions. One example of ensuring alignment is through regular team meetings or huddles where goals, priorities, and strategies are discussed. These meetings provide an opportunity for team members to ask questions, share insights, and ensure that everyone is working toward the same objectives.

Let's dive into an example to tie it all together:

Imagine a multinational corporation launching a new product globally. The sales team is spread across different regions, each responsible for a specific market. Effective communication plays a critical role in the success of this launch.

Keeping the Lines Open: *The sales team utilizes a project management tool like Trello or Asana to track progress and updates. They also schedule regular video conferences using Zoom to discuss strategy, address concerns, and provide updates on market developments.*

Fostering Transparency: *The sales manager sends out weekly email updates to the entire team, highlighting key achievements, challenges, and upcoming milestones. Additionally, they maintain an open-door policy, encouraging team members to voice their opinions and concerns openly.*

Ensuring Alignment: *Before the product launch, the sales leadership conducts a series of workshops to align the entire team on the product features, target markets, pricing strategy, and sales tactics. This ensures that every member of the team understands their role in achieving the overarching sales goals.*

By prioritizing effective communication, this sales team maximizes its chances of success in launching the new product globally.

Celebrate Diversity

Your global sales team is a melting pot of cultures, backgrounds, and perspectives. Embrace this diversity as a strength, not a weakness, and create an inclusive environment where everyone feels valued. Celebrating diversity within your global sales team can lead to numerous benefits, including increased creativity, innovation, and overall team performance. Here's how you can embrace diversity as a strength and foster an inclusive environment.

- **Cultural Awareness Training:** Provide cultural awareness training to all team members to help everyone understand and appreciate the nuances of different cultures represented within the team. For example, in a team where members come from various countries, understanding cultural differences in communication styles, negotiation tactics, and business etiquette can prevent misunderstandings and conflicts.
- **Language Skills:** Leverage the multilingual abilities of your team members to your advantage. In a sales context, having team members who can speak different languages can help in reaching out to diverse customer bases more effectively. For instance, if your team includes a member fluent in Mandarin, they can engage with clients in China more comfortably, leading to stronger relationships and increased sales.
- **Cultural Celebrations:** Encourage the celebration of cultural festivals and holidays within the team. This not only promotes a sense of belonging but also provides an opportunity for team members to share their traditions and customs with others. For example, hosting a potluck where team members bring dishes from their respective cultures can be a fun and enriching experience for everyone.
- **Diverse Perspectives:** Emphasize the importance of diverse perspectives in problem-solving and decision-making

processes. When faced with a challenge or opportunity, encourage team members to share their unique insights and approaches based on their backgrounds and experiences. This can lead to more creative solutions and better outcomes. For instance, a sales strategy that works well in one market may not be effective in another due to cultural differences, so having diverse perspectives can help tailor approaches accordingly.

- **Inclusive Policies:** Implement inclusive policies that accommodate the diverse needs of team members. This can include flexible work hours to accommodate different time zones, religious accommodation for holidays and observances, and ensuring accessibility for team members with disabilities. By creating a supportive environment where everyone feels valued and respected, you foster a culture of inclusion and belonging.
- **Recognition and Rewards:** Recognize and reward contributions from all team members, regardless of their background or cultural differences. Celebrate individual and team achievements openly and ensure that credit is given where it is due. This reinforces the idea that diversity is indeed a strength and that every team member's contribution is valuable.

By embracing diversity as a strength and creating an inclusive environment, you not only improve team morale and cohesion but also position your sales team for greater success in a global marketplace.

Don't Forget to Laugh

In the fast-paced world of global sales, a sense of humor can be your secret weapon. Whether you're navigating a language mix-up or braving a cultural faux pas, don't be afraid to laugh at yourself and keep things light. Incorporating humor into global sales can help build rapport, diffuse tense situations, and create memorable interactions with clients from different cultural backgrounds. Here are some examples that I could conjure.

- **Language Mix-Ups:** Imagine you're negotiating a deal with a client whose first language isn't English. During the conversation, they accidentally use a word that sounds similar to a profanity in English. Instead of ignoring it or letting it derail the conversation, you could playfully acknowledge the mix-up, saying something like, "Well, that's certainly one way to add some spice to our negotiation! Let's make sure we're on the same page here."
- **Cultural Faux Pas:** In some cultures, directness is valued, while in others, it can be seen as rude. If you unintentionally offend a client by being too direct, acknowledging the misstep with humor can help smooth things over. For example, you could say, "Oops, I think I just did the equivalent of accidentally stepping on your toes in this conversation. Let me take a step back and approach this from a different angle."
- **Virtual Meetings:** With the rise of remote work and virtual meetings, technical glitches are inevitable. If your video freezes at an awkward moment or your audio cuts out during an important point, rather than getting flustered, you can use humor to lighten the mood. For instance, you might say,

"Well, it seems even technology wants to keep us on our toes today. Let's take a moment to appreciate the unexpected pause and dive back in."

- **Cultural Differences in Humor:** Understanding the cultural context of humor is crucial when working with clients from diverse backgrounds. What may be funny in one culture could be misunderstood or even offensive in another. However, sharing light-hearted, universally relatable anecdotes or jokes can often bridge cultural gaps and foster camaraderie. Just ensure the humor is appropriate and respectful of cultural sensitivities.
- **Self-Deprecating Humor:** Don't be afraid to laugh at yourself! Sharing a humorous story about a mistake you made or an embarrassing moment can humanize you and make you more relatable to clients. It also shows humility and can help to build trust. Just be sure not to undermine your credibility in the process.

Incorporating humor into global sales requires sensitivity and tact, but when done right, it can be a powerful tool for building connections and navigating the complexities of cross-cultural communication. Remember, laughter is a universal language that can transcend barriers and leave a lasting impression.

Anchoring the Journey

As we bring this chapter to a close, remember that the journey of global sales is as much about the destinations we reach as it is about the adventures along the way. Embrace the challenges, savor the victories, and never lose sight of the human connections that lie at the heart of every sale. So, as we prepare to dock this chapter of our global sales voyage, let's not forget the sheer thrill of the journey itself. Just like a roller coaster ride, it's not just about reaching the end destination, but about screaming your lungs out and waving your arms in excitement along the twists and turns!

Embrace the challenges like a stubborn pickle jar, relish the victories like a kid with a trophy made of chocolate, and cherish those human connections like they're the last slice of pizza at a party. Now, as we set sail once more, let's not forget our trusty compass (or GPS, if you're feeling fancy) and our lucky socks. Because in the wild seas of global commerce, you never know when a lucky sock might just save the day!

Fair winds and following seas, my sales mates! May your ships be filled with lucrative deals, your emails be free of typos, and your coffee always be strong. Onward to new horizons, where the only limit is our imagination and maybe the occasional lack of Wi-Fi signal. But fear not, for where there's a will to close a sale, there's always a way!

So, hoist your sails, set your course, and let's sail forth into the sunset of endless possibilities. And remember, if all else fails, just smile, nod, and offer them a firm handshake. Works like a charm, every time!

8

BEYOND THE PITCH—NAVIGATING COMPLEX CUSTOMER INTERACTIONS

As someone embarking on or navigating through a sales career, you're likely aware that the path to success is rarely a straight line. Throughout my own journey in sales, I've encountered a myriad of challenges that have tested my skills, patience, and resilience. In sharing these scenarios with you, I aim to provide not only a glimpse into the complexities of the sales profession but also practical tips and strategies to overcome them. Navigating these situations requires a combination of sales skills, empathy, negotiation tactics, and problem-solving abilities.

In this compilation, I've outlined various scenarios that you may encounter in your sales career, ranging from budget constraints and tough competition to ethical dilemmas and cultural differences. Each situation presents its own unique set of obstacles, but with the right approach and mindset, they can all be navigated successfully.

I've also included some of my own experiences to offer real-world examples and insights into how these challenges can be tackled effectively. Whether you're a seasoned sales professional or just starting out, my hope is that these scenarios and tips will serve as valuable resources to help you navigate the ups and downs of the sales journey and ultimately achieve success. Here we go.

Budget Constraints

The customer wants a premium product but has a limited budget, putting the salesperson in a difficult position of trying to upsell without alienating the customer.

Ah, the classic conundrum of champagne taste on a beer budget! It's a situation that requires finesse, tact, and a touch of sales wizardry. Let's unpack this with some sage advice. Firstly, let's address the delicate dance of upselling without sending your customer running for the hills faster than you can say "discount." It's all about framing. Instead of focusing solely on the price, emphasize the value proposition of the premium product. Highlight its superior features, durability, and long-term benefits. After all, who doesn't want to feel like they're getting a steal of a deal on something that'll last a lifetime?

One effective strategy is to offer a tiered pricing structure. Present your premium product as the creme de la creme, but also have a mid-range option that offers a compromise between quality and affordability. This way, you're giving your customer the illusion of choice while gently nudging them toward the higher-end option.

Drawing from my own experiences in the field, I've found that building rapport is key to overcoming budget constraints. Take the time to really understand your customer's needs and preferences. Listen actively, ask probing questions, and tailor your recommendations accordingly. By demonstrating that you genuinely care about finding the best solution for them, you'll earn their trust and loyalty, making them more receptive to upselling.

Lastly, don't forget to sweeten the deal with some irresistible incentives. Whether it's a limited-time discount, a complimentary upgrade, or a tantalizing add-on, throwing in a little extra something can often tip the scales in your favor. Just be sure to frame it as a value-add rather than a desperate attempt to make a sale. In the end, it's all about striking the right balance between meeting your customer's needs and maximizing your sales potential. With a dash of charm, a dollop of empathy, and some strategic savvy, you'll be upselling like a pro in no time. Cheers to that!

Example: Let's say you're a salesperson at a high-end electronics store, and a customer comes in looking for a new laptop. They're eyeing the latest model with all the bells and whistles, but their budget is more aligned with a mid-range option.

You start by engaging them in conversation, asking about their needs and what they'll primarily be using the laptop for. As they explain that they need it for work and occasional gaming, you realize that the premium model would be perfect for their needs due to its powerful processor and graphics capabilities.

Instead of immediately pushing the premium model, you guide them through a comparison of the different options, highlighting the unique features of each. You emphasize the superior performance and durability of the premium model, but also point out that the mid-range option offers great value for their budget. To sweeten the deal, you mention a limited-time promotion where they can get a significant discount on accessories like a mouse, laptop bag, and antivirus software if they purchase the premium model. You also throw in an extended warranty as an added incentive for peace of mind.

Throughout the conversation, you sprinkle in some lighthearted humor to keep the mood relaxed and friendly. Maybe you make a joke about how the premium model is like the sports car of laptops, sure to make their colleagues green with envy.

By the end of the interaction, the customer feels like they've been given personalized attention and expert guidance. They appreciate the value proposition of the premium model and are delighted by the extra perks you've thrown in. In the end, they happily choose the premium option, feeling like they've scored a great deal without breaking the bank.

Competing Priorities

The customer has multiple projects or initiatives competing for attention and resources, making it challenging for the salesperson to prioritize their solution. The juggling act of competing priorities in the realm of sales—it's like being in a circus, except instead of juggling colorful balls, you're juggling the hopes and dreams of your customers, all the while trying to keep your own sanity intact.

So, picture this: You've got a customer who's the CEO of Multitasking Inc., with a to-do list longer than a CVS receipt. They've got projects coming out of their ears, initiatives popping up like mushrooms after rain, and resources spread thinner than butter on a cracker. How do you even begin to compete for attention in such a chaotic landscape?

First things first; you've got to understand their priorities better than they do themselves. Dive deep into their world, like a detective on a mission. What are their biggest pain points? What keeps them up at night, tossing and turning like a rotisserie chicken? Once you've cracked the code, you can tailor your solution to fit snugly into their whirlwind of priorities.

Next, it's time to get creative. Think outside the box, or heck, throw the box out altogether. Maybe your solution can actually help alleviate some of their other priorities. Turn yourself into the Swiss Army Knife of sales, with a tool for every occasion. But wait, there's more! Communication is key, my friend. Don't just send emails into the void and hope for the best. Pick up the phone, schedule a video call, or better yet, show up at their office with a bouquet of flowers and serenade them with your pitch (okay, maybe skip the serenade, but you get the idea). Building a personal connection can go a long way in a sea of competing priorities.

And finally, never underestimate the power of persistence. Rome wasn't built in a day, and neither is a successful sale. Keep chipping away, keep following up, and eventually, you'll break through the noise and emerge victorious. As for my own experiences, let me tell you, I've seen it all—from customers juggling so many priorities they might as well join the circus to salespeople pulling off feats of acrobatics to win them over. It's a wild ride, but with the right strategy and a sprinkle of humor, you can come out on top every time.

Let me share a real-world example from my experience working with a client in the technology sector.

Example: I once had a client who was the IT director for a medium-sized company undergoing a major digital transformation. They were in the midst of implementing new software systems, upgrading their hardware, and rolling out a new cybersecurity initiative—all while trying to keep the lights on for their day-to-day operations. Talk about juggling! To add to the chaos, they were bombarded with pitches from various vendors, each claiming to have the solution to their every problem. So, how did we stand out in this sea of competing priorities?

First, we took the time to truly understand their pain points and priorities. We scheduled multiple meetings, not just to talk about our product, but to listen to their challenges and concerns. By doing so, we were able to tailor our solution to address their most pressing needs, like streamlining their software systems to free up time for their IT team. Next, we got creative with our approach. Rather than just pitching our product as a standalone solution, we positioned it as a key component of their broader digital transformation strategy. We showed them how our software could integrate seamlessly with their existing systems, saving them time and resources in the long run.

But perhaps the most important factor was our communication strategy. We didn't just rely on emails and phone calls; we made an effort to build a personal connection with the IT director and his team. We took them out for coffee, invited them to industry events, and even went bowling together (because who doesn't love a good team-building activity?). And of course, we didn't give up at the first sign of resistance. We persisted, following up regularly and providing ongoing support even after the sale was made. In the end, our client not only became a loyal customer but also referred us to other companies in their network—a testament to the power of perseverance in the face of competing priorities.

So, there you have it—a real-world example of how to tackle competing priorities in sales with a mix of understanding, creativity, communication, and persistence. It's not always easy, but with the right approach, you can turn chaos into opportunity.

Lack of Decision-Making Authority

Dealing with a customer who lacks the authority to make purchasing decisions requires the salesperson to navigate complex decision-making hierarchies. The ol' "Decision-Making Dance"—a tango through the labyrinthine corridors of corporate hierarchies! Picture this, you're poised to seal the deal, armed with your best pitch and a dazzling smile, only to discover your contact has about as much purchasing power as a potted plant. Fear not, intrepid salesperson! Let's navigate this maze together, with a sprinkle of wit and wisdom.

First off, empathy is your best friend. Understand that your contact might be trapped in a bureaucratic labyrinth worthy of a Greek myth. They're probably dodging Cerberus and navigating the Minotaur's maze just to get a memo signed. So, tread lightly, for they are but mere mortals in the kingdom of corporate Olympus.

To tackle this challenge head-on, here are some strategies:

- **Play Detective:** Channel your inner Sherlock Holmes and unearth the decision-making hierarchy. Who holds the

Excalibur of authority? Is it the CEO, the CFO, or the elusive Director of Procurement? Ask probing questions disguised as friendly banter. "So, who else at your company is as fabulous as you are?"

- **Build Allies:** Forge alliances within the organization like a savvy diplomat. Your contact may not wield the scepter of power, but they sure know who does. Butter them up with compliments and maybe a sprinkle of flattery. "Your tie screams 'I mean business.' Do you think the CEO would like mine too?"
- **Educate and Elevate:** Sometimes, your contact might not realize the full scope of your offering. Educate them on how your solution can slay dragons and vanquish foes, elevating their status in the eyes of their superiors. "With our product, you'll be the hero of the next board meeting!"
- **Host a Summit:** Arrange a meeting of the minds, a gathering of the decision-making pantheon. Bring your contact along for the ride, making them feel like Zeus's favorite mortal. Bonus points if you can secure a lavish spread fit for the gods.
- **Patience, Grasshopper:** Rome wasn't built in a day, and neither is a sale in a complex organization. Exercise patience, but also persistence. Follow up like a gentle breeze, not a hurricane. "Just checking in to see if you've ascended Mount Olympus yet?"

Now, let me regale you with a tale from the annals of sales lore. Once, I found myself in a similar predicament, faced with a contact who seemed more lost than Odysseus in the Cyclops's cave. Through a delicate dance of diplomacy and determination,

I managed to unearth the decision-maker and secure the deal. Remember, dear salesperson, where there's a will, there's a commission!

So, fear not the labyrinth of corporate bureaucracy. Arm yourself with patience, wit, and a touch of charm, and you shall emerge victorious, laurels adorning your brow. Onward, noble sales warrior, and may the winds of fortune be ever in your favor!

Tough Competition

Facing fierce competition from other vendors offering similar products or services, makes it difficult for the salesperson to differentiate their offering. The fierce battlefield of commerce is like a gladiatorial arena where every salesperson is armed with their wits, charm, and a PowerPoint presentation. Facing off against rivals with similar offerings can make one feel like a lone samurai in a sea of clones.

First off, let's acknowledge the elephant in the room: ***differentiation***. If your product or service is swimming in the same pond as countless others, standing out becomes a game of strategic acrobatics. You don't want to be just another fish in the sea; you want to be the majestic narwhal with a unicorn-like horn that everyone admires. So, how does one transform into a narwhal in a sea of minnows? Here are a few tricks up the sleeve:

- **Know Thyself (and Thy Competition):** Sun Tzu said it best in *The Art of War*, "...know your enemy and know yourself...." Understanding what makes your offering unique and what your competitors are bringing to the table is key.

Conduct a thorough SWOT analysis (Strengths, Weaknesses, Opportunities, Threats) not just for your own company, but for your rivals as well. This will help you pinpoint areas where you can shine brighter than the rest.

- **Craft Your Unique Selling Proposition (USP):** Think of your USP as your superhero origin story. What makes you different? What makes you special? Maybe your product is faster, cheaper, or more eco-friendly. Whatever it is, shout it from the rooftops (or at least from your sales pitch).
- **Tell a Compelling Story:** People love stories. They're like catnip for the human brain. Instead of bombarding your prospects with technical specs and jargon, weave a narrative around your offering. Paint a picture of how it will solve their problems, make their lives easier, or turn them into heroes in their own right.
- **Go Beyond the Product:** Sometimes, it's not just about the product itself, but the experience you provide. Offer exceptional customer service, provide valuable content through blogs or webinars, or throw in some irresistible bonuses. Make buying from you not just a transaction, but an experience.
- **Build Relationships:** In a world where everyone's vying for attention, building genuine relationships can be your secret weapon. Be human, be authentic, and show your prospects that you genuinely care about their needs. Remember, people buy from people they like and trust.
- **Innovate Constantly:** The only constant in business is change. Keep an eye on emerging trends, listen to customer feedback, and be willing to adapt and evolve. Stagnation is the enemy of differentiation.

In my own experience, I've seen how a combination of these strategies can work wonders. I once worked with a tech startup that was entering a market saturated with big players. Instead of trying to compete head-on, we focused on our nimbleness and ability to tailor solutions to each client's unique needs. We emphasized our agility, personalized service, and innovative approach, and soon enough, we were winning deals left and right.

So, dear sales warrior, remember: In the battle for differentiation, creativity is your Excalibur and persistence is your shield. Arm yourself well, stay true to your uniqueness, and march forth with confidence. The sea of competition may be vast, but with the right strategy, you'll be the narwhal that reigns supreme.

Product Limitations

When a product or service has limitations that raise concerns for the customer, it's essential for the salesperson to address those objections with honesty and skill. Selling something with minor flaws is like offering a dented can of beans—the contents are still good, but it takes credibility, confidence, and the ability to steer the conversation toward what truly matters to help the customer see its value.

First off, acknowledge the elephant in the room. Pretending those limitations don't exist is like trying to hide a pimple with a tiny band-aid; it's just not going to work. Instead, embrace them like a quirky feature. "Sure, our product might not be able to make you breakfast in bed, but it can certainly help you organize your chaotic mornings!" Next, turn those limitations into selling points. It's all about perspective, my friend. Maybe your product doesn't have all the bells and whistles of its competitors, but hey, it's simpler, more streamlined, like the minimalist of the product world. "Why drown in a sea of features when you can sail smoothly with just what you need?"

Then, offer solutions or workarounds. You're not just a salesperson, you're a problem-solver extraordinaire. Got a product with a shorter battery life? Throw in a portable charger and call it a power-packed bundle! "Think of it as a built-in excuse to take a break and recharge—both you and your device!" Confidence sells like hotcakes on a Sunday morning. If you believe in your product, your customers will too. Own those limitations like they're part of your master plan. "Sure, it's not perfect, but perfection is overrated anyway. Embrace the quirks—they're what make life interesting!"

<u>Example:</u> Back in my digital assistant days, I had a colleague who was selling a smartphone with a camera that wasn't quite up to par with the latest and greatest. Instead of dodging the issue, he embraced it head-on. He highlighted the phone's affordability, emphasized its sleek design and user-friendly interface, and offered tips on how customers could still capture Instagram-worthy shots with a little creativity. And you know what? He ended up selling more phones than the guy with the fancy camera but zero personality.

So, there you have it—tackle product limitations like a pro. Embrace, spin, solve, charm. Rinse and repeat until you're selling like a seasoned pro.

Changing Requirements

The customer's needs or requirements evolve during the sales process, forcing the salesperson to adapt their approach and solution accordingly. The ever-shifting sands of customer requirements is a challenge as timeless as trying to keep up with the latest Kardashian drama. But fear not, intrepid salesperson, for in this dynamic dance of needs and wants lies an opportunity to showcase your adaptability and finesse.

Firstly, let's face the challenge. Changing requirements are about as surprising as finding a Starbucks in a hipster neighborhood. They're bound to happen. So, instead of bemoaning the universe for its fickleness, let's embrace the chaos and turn it to our advantage.

One tried and true strategy is to establish clear lines of communication with the customer from the get-go. Think of it as setting up a hotline directly to their ever-evolving wishlist. Regular check-ins and updates ensure you're not caught off guard by sudden shifts in requirements, much like how checking the weather forecast prevents you from getting soaked in a surprise rainstorm.

Another trick up your sleeve is to maintain flexibility in your approach. Just like a seasoned chef adjusts their recipe based on the ingredients at hand, a savvy salesperson tailors their solution to meet the customer's changing needs. Remember, rigidity is about as helpful as a snorkel in the Sahara.

Now, onto the art of persuasion. When faced with shifting requirements, it's crucial to highlight the benefits of your solution in a way that resonates with the customer's evolving priorities. Think of yourself as a smooth-talking chameleon, effortlessly blending your pitch to match the colors of their shifting landscape. But perhaps the most potent weapon in your arsenal is empathy. Put yourself in the customer's shoes and genuinely understand their motivations and concerns.

As for my own experiences, let's just say I've seen my fair share of curveballs thrown my way. But each twist and turn only served to sharpen my skills and reinforce the importance of adaptability in the world of sales. Remember, in the battle of wits between salesperson and changing requirements, the adaptable always emerge victorious.

Example: So, in the world of technology sales, where the pace of change makes a Formula 1 race look like a leisurely stroll in the park, let's explore my own experience. In my years navigating the fast-paced world of tech sales, I've encountered my fair share of plot twists. One memorable instance involved pitching a state-of-the-art project management tool to a potential client. Everything seemed to be going swimmingly until they dropped the bombshell—their needs had shifted, and they now required a solution tailored specifically to remote team collaboration.

Instead of breaking into a cold sweat, I saw this as an opportunity to showcase my adaptability and creativity. I swiftly organized a meeting with the client to understand their new requirements in-depth. Listening attentively to their vision for a remote-friendly platform, I absorbed every detail like a sponge. Armed with this valuable insight, I mobilized my team with lightning speed. We pivoted our approach and revamped our project management tool to align with the client's evolving needs. It was a whirlwind of brainstorming sessions, late-night coding marathons, and rapid iterations.

Finally, the moment of truth arrived. We unveiled the enhanced version of our tool, tailored specifically for remote team collaboration. The client was impressed, to say the least. Within no time, we were finalizing the deal and celebrating a hard-earned victory. Reflecting on this experience, I realized the power of adaptability and agility. By embracing change and leveraging it to our advantage, we not only secured a crucial sale but also strengthened our relationship with the client. It's a testament to the importance of staying nimble and innovative in an ever-evolving industry.

Remember this, in the face of changing requirements, adaptability is your greatest asset. Embrace the challenge, trust in your abilities, and turn every twist and turn into an opportunity for success.

Time Constraints

The customer needs a solution urgently but has a tight deadline or implementation schedule, putting pressure on the salesperson to expedite the sales process. The infamous time crunch is where urgency meets opportunity, and salespeople find themselves walking a tightrope between efficiency and effectiveness.

Picture this, you've got a customer who needs a solution yesterday, and your sales process suddenly feels like a race against the clock. It's like trying to build a sandcastle during high tide—challenging, but not impossible. First things first, keep your cool.

Panicking won't make time slow down, unfortunately. Instead, let's strategize like the seasoned sales pros we are.

- **Prioritize Like a Pro:** When time is of the essence, it's all about ruthless prioritization. Identify the key needs and pain points of your customer and focus on addressing those first. It's like a game of sales Jenga—carefully remove the non-essential blocks without toppling the tower of your pitch.
- **Streamline the Process:** Efficiency is your best friend in a time crunch. Streamline your sales process by cutting out any unnecessary steps or red tape. If your sales strategy doesn't spark joy or lead to a sale, it's gotta go.
- **Set Clear Expectations:** Transparency is key when the time is tight. Be upfront with your customer about the timeline and what can realistically be achieved. It's better to underpromise and overdeliver than to make empty promises and leave your customer disappointed. Remember, honesty is the best policy—even in sales.
- **Leverage Resources:** Don't be afraid to call in reinforcements. Whether it's enlisting the help of your team members or tapping into resources provided by your company, utilize every tool at your disposal to expedite the sales process. It's like assembling a sales Avengers team—each member bringing their unique skills to save the day.
- **Stay Nimble:** Flexibility is your secret weapon in a time crunch. Be prepared to adapt and pivot as needed to meet the evolving needs of your customer. Think of it as a sales salsa dance—quick on your feet and ready to spin in any direction necessary.

Example: I once had a client who needed a custom solution within a ridiculously tight deadline. Instead of panicking, we huddled up, streamlined our process, and worked around the clock to deliver a solution that not only met their needs but exceeded their expectations. It was a testament to the power of teamwork, agility, and a healthy dose of caffeine.

So, the next time you find yourself facing a time crunch in sales, remember these tips, keep your sense of humor intact, and tackle the challenge head-on. After all, a little pressure never hurt anyone—it just makes the victory that much sweeter.

Trust Issues

The customer is skeptical or mistrustful of salespeople in general, making it challenging for the salesperson to build rapport and establish credibility. The age-old battle between salespeople and the trust-wary customer! It's like trying to convince a cat to take a bubble bath—challenging, but not impossible. Let's explore this delicate dance, shall we?

Firstly, it's essential to understand why trust issues exist. Maybe they had a bad experience with a pushy salesperson in the past, or perhaps they've just binge-watched too many episodes of *The Office* and are convinced all salespeople are like Dwight Schrute. Whatever the reason, it's up to you to break through that skepticism and prove you're not just another "overly enthusiastic" paper salesman. One effective strategy is to lead with authenticity. Show sincere interest in the customer's needs and concerns, and be completely transparent—like a freshly cleaned window. When you're honest and upfront from the start, it's much harder for the customer to stay skeptical.

Another tactic is to build credibility through social proof. Share success stories or testimonials from satisfied customers. It's like bringing along your entourage to a job interview—they vouch for you, and suddenly you're the hottest candidate in the room. And remember, persistence pays off. Building trust takes time, like trying to teach your pet dog to fetch. Be patient, stay consistent, and eventually, you'll break through those trust barriers like a superhero crashing through a flimsy plywood wall.

<u>Example:</u> I've encountered my fair share of clients with trust issues. One particular instance stands out in my memory; I was part of a team tasked with selling a new cybersecurity solution to a large corporation. The client, understandably, was skeptical about investing in yet another software promising to protect their sensitive data. They had been burned in the past by flashy sales pitches that failed to deliver on their promises. To overcome this challenge, our approach was twofold—we focused on building trust through transparency and demonstrating the effectiveness of our solution through real time examples.

Firstly, we took the time to truly understand the client's concerns and pain points. We listened attentively as they expressed their frustrations with previous cybersecurity solutions and the repercussions they had faced due to breaches. By showing empathy and understanding, we began to break down the walls of skepticism.

Next, we provided concrete evidence of the effectiveness of our solution. We shared case studies and testimonials from other clients who had experienced significant improvements in their cybersecurity posture after implementing our software. Additionally, we offered to conduct a live demonstration of our solution, showing the client firsthand how it could protect their network from potential threats. Throughout the sales process, we kept up a light-hearted atmosphere . We cracked jokes about how to keep our wits to stay one step ahead of cybercriminals. This helped to humanize our team and build rapport with the client, making them more comfortable with the idea of working with us.

Ultimately, our efforts paid off. The client was impressed by our transparency, the evidence of our solution's effectiveness, and our ability to connect with them on a personal level. They decided to move forward with implementing our cybersecurity solution, and we were able to forge a strong and trusting relationship with them. This experience taught me the importance of addressing trust issues head-on in the technology industry. By being transparent, providing evidence of value, injecting humor into interactions, and building rapport with clients, even the most skeptical customers can be won over.

Cultural Differences

Dealing with customers from different cultural backgrounds requires the salesperson to navigate cultural nuances and communication styles effectively. The delightful dance of cultural differences in sales! Picture this, you're a salesperson, armed with charm and wit, ready to conquer the global marketplace.

But hold on, you're not just selling widgets, you're selling across cultural boundaries. It's like salsa dancing through a minefield of misunderstandings, but fear not, for I shall be your guide through this exotic adventure!

Firstly, let's talk about the importance of understanding cultural nuances. It's not just about knowing which hand to shake or whether to bow or curtsy (although those can be handy skills). It's about grasping the deeper layers of communication styles, social norms, and values that shape your customer's worldview. For instance, in some cultures, directness is prized, while in others, it's considered rude. So, when you're pitching your product, you might need to adjust your approach accordingly. Instead of going straight for the hard sell, you might want to start with some polite small talk to break the ice. But beware the pitfalls of humor across cultures. What's hilarious in one culture might fall flat or, worse, offend in another. So, tread lightly and always be sensitive to your audience.

Now, onto practical tips and strategies. One golden rule: Do your homework. Research your target culture's customs, etiquette, and taboos. It'll show that you respect and value their way of doing things. Plus, it's a great conversation starter. People love it when you take an interest in their culture.

Next, adapt your communication style. If you're dealing with a culture that values hierarchy, like Japan, show respect for authority and avoid being overly familiar. On the flip side, if you're selling to a more egalitarian culture, like Sweden, keep it casual and egalitarian. And never underestimate the power of language. If you can speak your customer's language—even just a few phrases—it can work wonders. It shows effort and sincerity, and it breaks down linguistic barriers like a champ.

I did exactly that in my sales deal in China. The little effort from my side—learning a little Mandarin for a basic exchange of pleasantries—paid off; we closed the deal happily.

Example: I was working as a sales representative for a tech company, and we had our eyes set on expanding into the vibrant markets of Southeast Asia.

One memorable encounter took place during a business trip to Singapore. I was meeting with a potential client, a local tech startup with ambitious growth plans. Now, Singapore is a melting pot of cultures, with influences from China, India, Malaysia, and beyond, so I knew I had to tread carefully to make a lasting impression. As I entered the meeting room, I noticed the subtle cues of hierarchy at play—a respectful bow from the junior staff and deferential nods from the senior executives. Drawing from my research, I reciprocated with a polite bow and addressed the CEO with the appropriate level of formality.

But it was during our presentation that the real magic happened. I had prepared a tailored pitch that highlighted how our software could streamline their operations and boost efficiency. However, I also knew that in Singapore, relationships matter as much as the product itself. So, I squeezed in some anecdotes and humor to lighten the mood, drawing parallels between our shared love of food (who can resist the allure of chili crab?) and the seamless integration of our software into their workflow. The room erupted in laughter, and I could sense a shift in energy as rapport began to form.

After the meeting, we continued our discussions over a sumptuous meal of laksa, exchanging stories and forging a deeper connection. In the end, it wasn't just about the features and benefits of our product—it was about building trust and understanding across cultural divides. Months later, I received the news that we had secured the deal with the Singaporean startup. It was a testament to the power of cultural sensitivity in sales and the importance of connecting on a human level, no matter the industry or geography.

That experience taught me valuable lessons that I carry with me to this day: do your homework, adapt your approach, and above all, never underestimate the universal language of laughter. In conclusion, navigating cultural differences in sales is like mastering the art of origami—delicate, precise, and occasionally fraught with peril. But with the right mix of preparation and adaptability, you can fold those cultural barriers into beautiful works of salesmanship.

Unclear Value Proposition

Here, the customer struggles to see the value proposition of the product or service being offered, requiring the salesperson to articulate the benefits clearly and persuasively. The struggle of unclear value proposition is like trying to sell ice to an Eskimo without explaining why they need it. But fear not, for every murky proposition can be clarified with the right blend of clarity and persuasion.

First things first, let's address the root of the issue—why is the value proposition as clear as pea souper in the first place? It could be a case of overly complex messaging, vague promises, or perhaps the product/service simply isn't solving a problem that the customer perceives they have. It's like trying to sell a map to someone who doesn't know they're lost.

So, how do we dig ourselves out of this value proposition quicksand? Here are some practical tips.

- **Know Thy Customer:** Understand your audience inside and out. What keeps them up at night? What are their pain points? Speak their language and tailor your value proposition to address their specific needs. It's like offering a refreshing glass of lemonade on a scorching summer day—you know they're thirsty for it!
- **Simplify, Simplify, Simplify:** Strip away the jargon and cut through the fluff. Your value proposition should be crystal clear and easy to understand, like a neon sign on a foggy night. If you can't explain it to your grandma in a way that makes her nod in comprehension, it's back to the drawing board.
- **Paint a Vivid Picture:** Use storytelling to illustrate how your product or service can transform the customer's life. People love a good yarn, especially if they're the hero at the end of it. Show them how your offering is the shining sword they need to slay their dragons.
- **Provide Social Proof:** Nothing speaks louder than satisfied customers. Share testimonials, case studies, or even better, let your happy clients do the talking for you. It's like having

a cheering squad on standby, ready to vouch for your awesomeness.

- **Differentiate:** What sets you apart from the competition? Highlight your unique selling points like a peacock flaunting its feathers. Whether it's superior quality, unbeatable prices, or unparalleled customer service, make sure your value proposition stands out in a sea of sameness.
- **Demo Time:** Sometimes, seeing is believing. Offer free trials or demos to let potential customers experience the magic firsthand. It's like letting them test drive a shiny new sports car—you know they'll be hooked once they feel the wind in their hair.

In my line of work, I've seen countless value propositions stumble out of the gate, only to soar to new heights with a little TLC. Take, for example, a software company I once worked with. Their product was a game-changer in the industry, but their value proposition was buried under a pile of technical mumbo-jumbo. By repositioning their messaging to focus on the time-saving benefits for busy professionals and backing it up with glowing testimonials, they saw a dramatic increase in conversions.

<u>Example:</u> In the realm of technology, a clear and compelling value proposition can make or break a product's success. Let me share an experience from my time working with a startup in the software-as-a-service (SaaS) industry. The company had developed a revolutionary project management tool designed to streamline collaboration and boost productivity for remote teams. However, despite its innovative features, they were struggling to convey its value proposition effectively to potential customers.

Upon diving into the issue, we identified several factors contributing to the unclear value proposition such as:

- **Technical Jargon Overload:** The initial marketing materials were drowning in technical terminology, leaving potential users scratching their heads instead of nodding in agreement.
- **Lack of Tangible Benefits:** While the features of the tool were impressive, we weren't effectively communicating how it would directly address the pain points of our target audience and improve their workflow.
- **Competitive Landscape:** The project management space was crowded with established players, making it crucial for us to differentiate our offering and showcase its unique value.

To tackle these challenges, we implemented a multifaceted strategy that involved:

- **Simplified Messaging:** We revamped our website copy and marketing materials to focus on the core benefits of the tool in plain language. Instead of listing features, we highlighted how it would save time, reduce communication overhead, and increase team collaboration.
- **Customer Stories:** We reached out to early adopters and gathered their feedback and success stories. By showcasing real-world examples of how the tool had transformed their workflows and boosted productivity, we provided social proof of its effectiveness.
- **Competitive Analysis:** We conducted an in-depth analysis of competing products to identify gaps and opportunities. By emphasizing our unique features, such as seamless integration with popular productivity tools and advanced reporting

capabilities, we positioned our tool as the superior choice in the market.

- **Free Trial Offer:** We introduced a free trial option, allowing potential customers to experience the benefits of the tool firsthand without commitment. This hands-on approach proved to be highly effective in converting leads into paying customers.

As a result of these efforts, we saw a significant improvement in customer engagement and conversion rates. Our revamped value proposition resonated with our target audience, leading to increased interest in and adoption of the product.

In conclusion, navigating the murky waters of an unclear value proposition in the technology industry requires a strategic approach focused on simplifying messaging, highlighting tangible benefits, differentiating from competitors, and providing real-world proof of value. Remember, clarity is key and persuasion is power. With these tools in your arsenal, you'll have those customers singing your praises in no time.

Risk Aversion

A risk-averse customer is hesitant to commit to a purchase, requiring the salesperson to mitigate perceived risks and provide assurances. Now, let's understand our risk-averse friend. They're the type who bring an umbrella to a sunny picnic, just in case. They're not ready to leap into the unknown without a safety net made of assurances and guarantees. So, how do we win them over? Well, it's all about building trust and providing comfort blankets for their anxious souls. Here are some practical tips.

- **Offer a Safety Net:** Imagine you're selling parachutes. You wouldn't just hand them a backpack and say, "Trust me, it'll work!" You'd explain the rigorous testing, the decades of experience, and maybe throw in a few reassuring stories of successful landings.
- **Showcase Social Proof:** People love to follow the herd, so herd them toward your product with testimonials, reviews, and success stories. Make them feel like they're joining an exclusive club of satisfied customers.
- **Money-Back Guarantees:** Nothing says "I believe in my product" like a good ol' money-back guarantee. It's like saying, "Hey, if this doesn't work out, no hard feelings, we'll still be pals."
- **Head-On Address Concerns:** Don't tiptoe around their fears like a cat avoiding a puddle. Dive right in and address their concerns with facts, figures, and a sprinkle of charm. Show them you've got nothing to hide.
- **Be Their Guide:** Remember, you're not just selling a product, you're selling a solution to their problem. Paint yourself as their trusty guide through the treacherous waters of decision-making. Throw them a lifeline and reassure them that you've got their back.

Now, let me regale you with a tale from the trenches of salesmanship.

<u>Example:</u> A few years back, I was working as a sales representative for a software company that specialized in cloud-based solutions for small businesses. We had developed a cutting-edge software suite that promised to streamline operations, increase efficiency,

and boost productivity. However, convincing skeptical business owners to make the leap into the cloud wasn't always easy.

One particular prospect stands out in my memory. Let's call him Mr. Smith. Mr. Smith was the owner of a small manufacturing company, and he was hesitant to commit to our software due to concerns about data security and reliability. He was a classic example of a risk-averse customer, reluctant to embrace new technology without ironclad assurances. So, armed with a healthy dose of product knowledge, I set out to win Mr. Smith over. Here's how I tackled his concerns.

- **Education:** I started by educating Mr. Smith about the robust security measures we had in place, including encryption, regular backups, and stringent access controls. I explained how our software had been rigorously tested and was trusted by thousands of businesses worldwide.
- **Demonstration:** Next, I offered to provide Mr. Smith with a personalized demonstration of our software. I walked him through the user interface, highlighting key features and demonstrating how our solution could address his specific pain points and improve his business processes.
- **Case Studies:** I shared success stories and case studies from other manufacturing companies that had implemented our software with great success. Hearing real-world examples of how our solution had helped similar businesses overcome their challenges helped to alleviate Mr. Smith's concerns and build trust.
- **Trial Period:** To further mitigate Mr. Smith's perceived risk, I proposed a trial period during which he could test our software

with no obligation. This allowed him to see firsthand how our solution could benefit his business without committing to a long-term contract upfront.

- **Personalized Support:** Finally, I assured Mr. Smith that our dedicated customer support team would be there to assist him every step of the way, from initial setup to ongoing maintenance and troubleshooting. Knowing that he wouldn't be left to fend for himself in case of any issues gave him added peace of mind.

In the end, my efforts paid off, and Mr. Smith decided to take the plunge and implement our software in his manufacturing company. Seeing the tangible benefits of our solution firsthand, coupled with the personalized support and assurances we provided, helped to alleviate his concerns and win him over as a satisfied customer.

This experience taught me the importance of understanding and addressing the concerns of risk-averse customers. By providing education, demonstrations, social proof, trial periods, and personalized support, sales professionals can effectively mitigate perceived risks and build trust with even the most cautious of prospects. So, my friend, fear not the risk-averse customer, for they are but a challenge waiting to be conquered.

Internal Politics

Dealing with internal stakeholders within the customer's organization who have conflicting agendas or priorities, makes it challenging to gain consensus and move the sales process forward. The tangled web of internal politics within a customer's organization where conflicting agendas dance the tango of office politics, makes consensus feel like herding cats through a maze.

Firstly, let's acknowledge that navigating this labyrinth requires a delicate balance of diplomacy, strategic thinking, and perhaps a touch of psychological acumen. Picture yourself as a sales samurai, armed not with a sword but with a keen understanding of human behavior and organizational dynamics. Here are some battle-tested strategies to emerge victorious.

- **Know Thy Players:** Before charging headlong into the fray, take the time to map out the power dynamics within the organization. Who are the key decision-makers? Who holds sway over them? And most importantly, who harbors vendettas against whom? It's like plotting a geopolitical map, only with less geopolitics and more water cooler gossip.
- **Build Alliances:** In the game of thrones that is corporate life, allies are worth their weight in gold-pressed platinum. Identify potential allies among the stakeholders and cultivate relationships with them. Offer value, be it in the form of insights, solutions to their pain points, or simply a sympathetic ear for their office woes. Remember, a shared enemy can often make the strongest bonds.
- **Speak Their Language:** Each stakeholder has their own agenda, priorities, and preferred communication style. Tailor your pitch accordingly. If the CFO's eyes glaze over at the mention of technical jargon, speak in the language of ROI and bottom-line impact. If the marketing director is allergic to spreadsheets, paint a vivid picture of how your solution

will revolutionize their campaigns. Good to remember that flexibility is key.

- **Manage Expectations:** Sometimes, gaining consensus is less about changing minds and more about managing expectations. Be transparent about what your solution can and cannot deliver. Under-promise and over-deliver—it's the oldest trick in the book, but like a fine wine or a classic rock ballad, it never goes out of style.
- **Play the Long Game:** I know I keep repeating this but, Rome wasn't built in a day, and neither is a consensus among stakeholders. Be patient, persistent, and above all, resilient. Rome also wasn't built by panicking at the first sign of trouble. Keep your eye on the prize and remember that every setback is just a plot twist in the epic saga of corporate life.

Once, I found myself in the midst of a sales process that resembled a Shakespearean tragedy, complete with warring factions and dramatic monologues. By carefully applying the strategies outlined above, I managed to broker a fragile peaceful setup among the stakeholders and emerge victorious. It was a triumph of diplomacy and strategy.

<u>Example:</u> Allow me to share an anecdote from my experience where navigating internal politics was as crucial as writing code or designing interfaces. In a previous role, I was leading a sales team tasked with selling a cutting-edge software solution to a large multinational corporation. The technology promised to streamline their operations, increase efficiency, and ultimately save them a boatload of money—a win-win proposition if ever there was one.

However, as we delved deeper into the sales process, it became apparent that gaining consensus among the various stakeholders was not going to be easy. The IT department, concerned about integration challenges and potential disruptions to their existing systems, was hesitant to commit. The finance department, while intrigued by the promise of cost savings, was wary of the upfront investment required. And the marketing department, well, they seemed more interested in debating the merits of the latest viral meme than in discussing software solutions.

Undeterred, I spent countless hours meeting with each stakeholder individually, listening to their concerns, and tailoring my pitch to address their specific needs. To the IT department, I emphasized our seamless integration process and the robust support infrastructure we offered. To the finance department, I presented a detailed ROI analysis, complete with projections of cost savings over time. And to the marketing department, I ... well, I may have slipped in a meme or two to lighten the mood.

But perhaps the most crucial aspect of my strategy was building alliances within the organization. I identified champions for our solution in each department—individuals who saw the potential benefits and were willing to advocate on our behalf. By aligning ourselves with these allies, we were able to gradually chip away at the resistance within the organization and build momentum toward consensus.

Of course, it wasn't all smooth sailing. There were setbacks and challenges along the way, moments when it seemed like the deal might fall through altogether. But by remaining patient, persistent, and adaptable, we ultimately succeeded in gaining buy-in from all the key stakeholders and closing the deal.

Looking back on that experience, I'm reminded of the old adage that sales is as much about people as it is about product. In the world of technology, where innovation moves at the speed of light and disruption is the name of the game, the ability to navigate internal politics and build consensus can be the difference between success and failure. And while it may not always be easy or glamorous, the rewards of overcoming those challenges and seeing your vision become reality are more than worth the effort.

Scope Creep

Here, the customer keeps adding new requirements or features to the project scope without a corresponding increase in budget or timeline, putting strain on the salesperson to manage expectations. The notorious beast known as scope creep is the bane of every project manager's existence! It's like trying to tame a wild horse that keeps growing extra legs every time you turn your back. But fear not, for I come bearing the tools of knowledge and the armor of experience to combat this unruly creature!

Firstly, let's address the root cause—the customer's insatiable appetite for more features without considering the poor budget and timeline already in place. It's like being at an all-you-can-eat buffet and still wanting more when you've already filled your plate to the brim!

But I digress. Here are some practical strategies to rein in scope creep.

- **Establish Clear Boundaries:** Make sure the project scope is clear. Define what's included and what's not.
- **Change Control Process:** Implement a robust change control process that requires any new requirements to go through a formal approval process.
- **Educate the Customer:** Sometimes, customers don't realize the impact of their requests on the project's budget and timeline. Educate them gently but firmly.
- **Negotiate Trade-offs:** When faced with new requirements, negotiate trade-offs. If they want to add a feature, they may need to sacrifice another or extend the timeline.
- **Document Everything:** Keep detailed records of all discussions and agreements to avoid any "he said, she said" scenarios later. Documentation prevents embarrassing situations.
- **Underpromise, Overdeliver:** When setting expectations, err on the side of caution. It's better to surprise the customer with early delivery or extra features than to disappoint them with delays and additional costs.
- **Build Buffer Time and Budget:** Factor in some wiggle room in your timeline and budget for unforeseen changes. This will keep you stress-free in some aspects at least.

<u>Example:</u> In a previous role, I was tasked with overseeing the development of a mobile application for a client in the healthcare sector. We had meticulously outlined the project scope, detailing the features, functionalities, and timeline. However, as development progressed, the client began to express a desire for additional features they believed were crucial for the success of the app.

One such feature was the integration of a complex telehealth module that would allow patients to schedule virtual appointments with healthcare providers. While this was undoubtedly valuable, it was not initially included in the project scope and would require significant additional development time and resources. Recognizing the potential for scope creep, I immediately scheduled a meeting with the client to discuss their new requirements. I began by reaffirming the importance of sticking to the agreed-upon scope to ensure timely delivery and budget adherence. However, I also empathized with their need for the telehealth functionality and proposed a solution.

Instead of outright rejecting the request, I suggested a phased approach. We would prioritize the core features of the app for the initial release, ensuring a timely launch to market. Then, we would incorporate the telehealth module in a subsequent update, allowing us to allocate the necessary resources without derailing the project timeline. Additionally, I highlighted the potential benefits of this approach, such as gathering user feedback from the initial release to inform the development of the telehealth module and ensuring a more polished and refined final product.

By effectively managing the client's expectations, negotiating trade-offs, and proposing a strategic solution, we were able to mitigate the impact of scope creep and maintain control over the project. In the end, we delivered a successful mobile application that met the client's needs while staying within budget and timeline constraints. This example underscores the importance of proactive communication, flexibility, and strategic decision-making in navigating scope creep.

Payment Issues

Payment issues can mean the customer encounters financial difficulties or delays in processing payments, impacting the salesperson's ability to close the deal or receive commission. This is the classic dance of finance and sales, where the tango of payment processing often takes unexpected twists and turns. It's like hitting a sudden pothole on a smooth road to success.

Now, let's unpack this conundrum like a seasoned detective, shall we? First off, financial difficulties can be as unpredictable as British weather—one moment it's sunny skies, the next, you're caught in a downpour without an umbrella. Similarly, payment delays are like those annoying traffic jams on a Monday morning—you're stuck, and there's no easy way out. But fear not, there are strategies aplenty to navigate these treacherous waters. Here are a few tricks up my sleeve.

- **Build Strong Relationships:** Much like a well-brewed cup of tea, relationships need time to brew. Establishing trust and rapport with your clients can make navigating payment issues smoother. A loyal client is more likely to communicate openly about financial snags.
- **Clarify Terms and Conditions:** Just like reading the fine print on a contract, clarifying payment terms upfront can save you from future headaches. Ensure your client understands the payment schedule and any penalties for late payments.
- **Offer Flexible Payment Options:** Think of it as a buffet—the more options, the merrier. Providing various payment methods, such as installment plans or online transfers, gives

clients flexibility and may help them overcome financial hurdles.

- **Follow Up Diligently:** Persistence pays off, quite literally. Gentle reminders about pending payments can nudge clients into action. However, remember to maintain professionalism and avoid becoming a nagging nuisance.
- **Have a Plan B (and C):** Expect the unexpected, like a true Boy Scout. Anticipate potential payment issues by having backup plans in place. This could involve securing alternative sources of funding or renegotiating payment terms if necessary.

Once, in a distant digital realm, a savvy salesperson found himself in the midst of a payment quagmire. Instead of succumbing to despair, he employed the aforementioned strategies with finesse. By fostering open communication, offering flexibility, and maintaining a positive attitude, he managed to salvage the deal and secure his well-deserved commission.

Example: In the world of technology sales, payment issues can sometimes feel like bugs in an otherwise seamless system. A while back, I was working as a technology sales consultant for a software company. We had just closed a substantial deal with a promising client for our cutting-edge project management software. Everything seemed hunky-dory until it was time to collect payment.

As fate would have it, our client encountered unexpected financial difficulties due to a restructuring within their organization. This left them unable to fulfill their payment obligations according to our agreed-upon terms. Cue the panic button. However, armed with my trusty arsenal of sales strategies, I sprang into action. First, I reached out to our client to express understanding and offer support. By fostering open communication, I gained valuable insights into their financial predicament and established a foundation of trust.

Next, I proposed alternative payment options tailored to fit their new circumstances. This included flexible payment schedules and exploring financing options to alleviate their immediate cash flow challenges. Additionally, I collaborated closely with our finance team to devise a contingency plan. We explored the possibility of restructuring the payment terms while ensuring minimal impact on our company's cash flow. Through persistence, patience, and a dash of negotiation prowess, we were able to navigate the stormy seas of payment issues and salvage the deal. Not only did we secure the much-needed revenue, we also strengthened our relationship with the client, paving the way for future collaborations.

In hindsight, this experience reinforced the importance of adaptability and proactive communication in overcoming payment hurdles. By remaining agile and responsive to the client's needs, we turned a potential setback into a valuable learning opportunity and a testament to our resilience as sales professionals in the ever-evolving tech landscape.

So remember, while payment issues may seem like insurmountable obstacles, they are but mere bumps in the road to success. With a dash of charm, and a dollop of perseverance, you can overcome any financial hurdle that comes your way. So, chin up, chest out, and waltz through those payment woes like the suave sales virtuoso that you are!

Ethical Dilemmas

Ethical dilemmas happen when the customer requests unethical or questionable practices, putting the salesperson in a moral quandary. The classic ethical tightrope act of salesmanship is like juggling flaming swords while balancing on a unicycle made of ice—thrilling, yet potentially hazardous to one's integrity. Let's enter this moral maze with the confidence of an expert gamer. Let's say you're a salesperson, ready to conquer the world of commerce. But then, like a dark cloud on the horizon, you encounter a customer whose requests veer into murky ethical territory. Maybe they're asking you to cut corners, bend rules, or outright engage in practices that would make even a con artist blush. What's a savvy salesperson to do?

Firstly, let's acknowledge the gravity of the situation. Ethical dilemmas are like unwanted guests at a dinner party—they demand attention and ignoring them won't make them disappear. So, let's strategize.

- **Know Thy Ethical Compass:** Before diving headfirst into the sales battlefield, take some time to define your ethical boundaries. What are the non-negotiables for you? What values do you hold dear? Knowing where you stand on the moral spectrum will serve as your North Star in navigating tricky situations.
- **Arm Yourself with Knowledge:** Knowledge is power, my friend. Educate yourself on relevant laws, regulations, and company policies. This way, you'll be equipped to gracefully sidestep any ethically dubious requests with finesse and confidence.

- **Master the Art of Persuasion:** Sometimes, customers make unethical demands out of ignorance or misguided beliefs. Use your powers of persuasion to gently steer them toward the path of righteousness. Show them that ethical practices aren't just morally upright but also beneficial in the long run.
- **Offer Ethical Alternatives:** When faced with an unethical request, be prepared to offer alternative solutions that align with your moral compass. Get creative! Think outside the box and find win-win solutions that satisfy both the customer and your conscience.
- **Seek Guidance:** Don't be afraid to seek guidance from mentors, colleagues, or even your company's ethics committee. Sometimes, a fresh perspective can illuminate a path forward that you hadn't considered.

Now, here are some examples and experiences to add flavor to our ethical stew.

Example 1: Imagine you're a salesperson for a tech company, and a potential client asks you to manipulate data to make their product appear more appealing. Instead of succumbing to the dark side of data manipulation, you could offer to showcase the product's genuine strengths and provide transparent information to help the client make an informed decision. By staying true to your ethical principles, you not only preserve your integrity but also build trust with the client in the long run.

Example 2: In another scenario, let's say you work for a pharmaceutical company, and a customer pressurizes you to promote a medication for off-label use. Rather than risking your professional reputation and potentially endangering patients, you could educate the customer on the importance of adhering to FDA regulations and steer them toward approved uses of the medication. It's a win-win: you maintain your ethical integrity while also upholding public safety.

Example 3: Several years ago, during my tenure at a software development company, I found myself in a rather sticky situation. We were in the midst of negotiations with a potential client for a custom software project. Everything seemed to be going swimmingly until the client dropped a bombshell; they requested that we implement a backdoor into the software to allow for covert access to user data. Now, as someone deeply ingrained in the tech world, I knew all too well the implications of such a request. Implementing a backdoor would compromise user privacy and security, not to mention violate numerous ethical principles and potentially legal regulations. It was like being asked to build a Trojan horse and sneak it into the city gates under the guise of a gift.

In that moment, I felt the weight of responsibility on my shoulders. On one hand, there was the allure of a lucrative contract and the pressure to please the client. On the other hand, there was my integrity and the trust of the users whose data would be at risk. After careful consideration, I knew I couldn't in good conscience comply with the client's request. So, I mustered up my courage and delicately explained the ethical implications of their ask. I offered alternative solutions that would achieve their goals without compromising user privacy, such as implementing robust encryption protocols and strict access controls.

To my relief, the client ultimately understood and respected my stance. While they were initially disappointed, they appreciated the transparency and commitment to ethical principles. In the end, we reached a compromise that satisfied both parties, and the project proceeded without sacrificing integrity. This experience reinforced the importance of staying true to one's ethical compass, even in the face of temptation or pressure. It's a lesson that has stuck with me throughout my career, reminding me that integrity is non-negotiable, even in the cutthroat world of business.

Remember, ethical dilemmas are par for the course in the world of sales. But with the right mindset and strategies, you can navigate these choppy waters with grace and integrity.

Post-Sale Support

The customer is now expecting ongoing support or maintenance services beyond what was originally agreed upon. You've closed the deal, celebrated the win, and are just about to enjoy the satisfaction of a job well done—when suddenly, the customer drops the unexpected: "But what about ongoing support?"

Negotiating these additional terms or services can feel like walking a tightrope—requiring balance, focus, and a steady approach to avoid a misstep. But don't worry. I've got a toolkit of practical tips and strategies to help you navigate this tricky situation with confidence and control.

- **Set Clear Boundaries from the Get-Go:** Prevention is often the best medicine. Make sure your initial agreement is as crystal-clear as a freshly Windexed window. Outline precisely what's included in the sale and what falls outside its cozy confines. This way, there's less room for post-purchase haggling.

- **Create a Menu of Support Options:** Think of it as a support services buffet. Present your customer with a delectable array of support packages, each with its own price tag and level of service. This not only gives them choice but also helps set realistic expectations.
- **Embrace the Power of the Upsell:** This is the art of turning lemons into lemonade (and then selling that lemonade at a premium). Use the request for additional support as an opportunity to upsell. Maybe they just need a little extra handholding, or perhaps they'd benefit from a deluxe support package complete with 24/7 hotline access and a personal support unicorn. Get creative!
- **Leverage the Power of Reciprocity:** Remind your customer of all the wonderful things you've already done for them. Highlight the value you've brought to the table and gently nudge them to reciprocate by purchasing additional support services. After all, who can resist the allure of reciprocity?

Know When to Hold 'Em, Know When to Fold 'Em: Sometimes, despite your best efforts, the customer just won't budge. In these situations, it's crucial to know when to gracefully bow out. Don't waste precious time and energy trying to force a square peg into a round hole. Sometimes, it's better to cut your losses and move on to greener pastures. Once, I found myself locked in a post-sale support standoff with a particularly stubborn customer. No matter how much I tried to sweeten the deal, they remained steadfast in their refusal to pony up for additional services. In the end, I had to concede defeat and accept that some battles are simply not worth fighting.

Example: In the technology industry, post-sale support can often be a maze of intricacies, and navigating it requires a deft touch. Allow me to recount an experience from my own journey.

I was part of a sales team tasked with selling a comprehensive software solution to a mid-sized company. After weeks of tireless pitches, demos, and negotiations, we finally sealed the deal. The champagne flowed, and victory seemed assured. However, as the dust settled, the customer raised a concern: "What about ongoing support and maintenance?" Cue the collective groan from our sales team. It was a classic case of post-sale support expectations veering off into uncharted territory. But armed with wit and strategy, we embarked on a mission to turn this challenge into an opportunity.

We scheduled a meeting with the customer to discuss their support needs in detail. Drawing upon our expertise, we presented them with a menu of support options ranging from basic troubleshooting assistance to round-the-clock support with guaranteed response times. We emphasized the value of each tier and tailored our recommendations to suit their specific requirements. However, the customer remained hesitant, expressing concerns about the additional cost. Sensing an opportunity, we leveraged the power of reciprocity, reminding them of the extensive customization and training we had provided during the implementation phase. We highlighted the tangible benefits they had already reaped from our solution and positioned additional support as the logical next step in their journey toward success.

Ultimately, our persistence paid off. The customer recognized the value proposition we presented and agreed to invest in a premium support package. Not only did this secure a recurring revenue stream for our company, but it also strengthened our relationship with the customer, positioning us as a trusted partner rather than a mere vendor. This experience taught me the importance of proactive communication, creative problem-solving, and the art of the upsell in the realm of post-sale support. By approaching each challenge with agility and expertise, even the most daunting obstacles can be transformed into opportunities for mutual growth and success.

In conclusion, navigating the treacherous waters of post-sale support requires a delicate balance of tact and strategy. By setting clear boundaries, offering enticing support options, and knowing when to gracefully bow out, you can emerge victorious from even the most daunting negotiations. So go forth, dear salesperson, and may the winds of post-sale support blow ever in your favor! Remember, every challenge is an opportunity for growth and learning. Embrace them with confidence, adaptability, and a willingness to learn, and you'll be well-equipped to overcome any obstacle that comes your way.

9

THE MANAGERIAL METAMORPHOSIS—FROM SALES PRO TO FIRST-TIME MANAGER

As I sit down to write this chapter, I find myself reflecting on my own journey from being a salesperson to stepping into the role of a first-time manager. It's a transition filled with excitement, challenges, and a whole lot of learning. Through this chapter, I hope to share some insights and tips that can help you navigate this transition more smoothly. So, let's begin!

From Selling to Leading

Transitioning from a sales role to a managerial position is like switching gears in a fast-moving car. Suddenly, you're not just responsible for your own targets and performance but also for guiding a team toward success. I vividly remember the mix of emotions I felt when I first stepped into my manager's shoes—excitement, nervousness, and a tinge of imposter syndrome.

Imagine yourself cruising along the highway of your career, navigating the twists and turns of the sales landscape with precision and skill. As a salesperson, your primary focus is on hitting your individual targets, closing deals, and ensuring customer satisfaction. It's a high-energy, high-stakes environment where every negotiation, every pitch, could make or break your success. Then, suddenly, you're handed the keys to a different vehicle altogether—one with a larger engine, more seats, and a different set of controls. You're now in the driver's seat of a team, responsible not just for your own performance but for the collective success of those under your guidance. The transition is exhilarating, to say the least. There's a palpable sense of excitement as you envision the possibilities of leading a team to new heights of achievement. Yet, intertwined with that excitement is a healthy dose of nervousness—the awareness of the increased responsibilities and expectations that come with the managerial role.

And then there's the imposter syndrome—that nagging voice in the back of your mind whispering doubts about whether you're truly ready for this new challenge. After all, you've spent years perfecting your craft as a salesperson, but managing a team requires an entirely different skill set—one that you may not yet feel fully equipped to wield. But just as a skilled driver adapts to the nuances of a new vehicle, so too can you adapt to the demands of managerial leadership. It's a journey of growth, learning, and self-discovery—one that will undoubtedly have its share of bumps in the road, but also moments of exhilaration as you see your team flourish under your guidance. So, buckle up and embrace the ride. The transition from salesperson to manager may feel like switching gears in a fast-moving car, but with determination, resilience, and a willingness to learn, you'll navigate this new terrain with confidence and grace.

I recall one of my early team meetings where I attempted to inspire my sales team with a motivational speech I had meticulously prepared. However, halfway through, I stumbled over my words and ended up quoting a famous philosopher instead of a renowned business leader. The room fell silent, but then laughter erupted, breaking the tension. It was a humbling experience that taught me the importance of authenticity and humility in leadership. As I grappled with the intricacies of managerial responsibilities, I couldn't help but think back to my days in school. Managing a team felt like trying to create a complex science model or experiment—requiring careful calculation, strategic thinking, and the occasional leap of faith. So here are some of the challenges that you may face during this transition phase and some suggested solutions to help you along.

Challenges and Solutions

- **Building Credibility:** As a new manager, earning the trust and respect of your team can be daunting. One tip is to leverage your expertise as a former salesperson by offering valuable insights and support. Show your team that you understand the challenges they face and are committed to helping them succeed.

As a former salesperson turned manager, I've learned a thing or two about building credibility and rapport with my team. Let me share a little anecdote to illustrate how leveraging my sales expertise has helped me in this regard.

Picture this: It's my first week as a manager, and I can feel the nervous energy buzzing around the office like a swarm of caffeinated bees. My team members are eyeing me cautiously, probably wondering if I'm going to be the kind of manager who swoops in with a clipboard and a scowl. So, I decide to shake things up a bit. I gather everyone for a team meeting and start off with a casual, "Alright folks, let's cut to the chase. I know what it's like out there in the trenches because I've been there. I've battled through the wild jungles of sales, dodged metaphorical bullets, and emerged victorious ... most of the time." Cue some chuckles from the team. Humor is always a great icebreaker, right?

Then, I dive into some insights I've gained from my sales days. I share stories of deals gone wrong, clients from Mars (figuratively speaking, of course), and the art of turning a "no" into a "not right now, but maybe later." With each tale, I see nods of recognition and even a few raised eyebrows of intrigue. They're starting to see that I get it. I understand the struggles they face because I've been there myself. But I don't stop there. I make it clear that I'm not just here to reminisce about the glory days of sales past. No, I'm here to roll up my sleeves and help them tackle their challenges head-on. Whether it's crafting the perfect pitch, navigating tricky client negotiations, or simply lending an empathetic ear, I'm all in.

And you know what? Slowly but surely, that initial skepticism starts to melt away. My team begins to see me not just as a manager, but as a trusted ally in their corner.

So, if you're a new manager looking to earn the trust and respect of your team, don't be afraid to lean on your past experiences. Share your insights and above all, show them that you're in this together. Who knows? You might just find that building credibility isn't as daunting as it seems.

- **Balancing Friendships and Authority:** Many first-time managers struggle with finding the right balance between being friendly with their team members and asserting their authority.

Remember, you can be approachable while still setting clear expectations and boundaries.

As a first-time manager, finding the sweet spot between being chummy with my team and asserting authority felt like tiptoeing through a minefield in clown shoes. Picture this: I stroll into the office, ready to lead my team to greatness, only to find myself offering high-fives instead of setting deadlines. But here's the thing, being approachable doesn't mean turning into the office teddy bear. Take Steve, for instance. He's the kind of guy who'd rather turn a meeting into a stand-up comedy routine than discuss deadlines. So, when Steve waltzed in late for the umpteenth time, I had to put on my serious face (not my forte, mind you) and gently remind him of the importance of punctuality.

Sure, I could've cracked a joke about how he's running on "Steve time" or suggested he invest in a jetpack, but instead, I calmly laid down the law while keeping the atmosphere light. Strike that perfect balance, and you'll find your team respecting your authority without fearing a humorless boss lurking in the shadows.

Remember, being friendly doesn't mean being a pushover. So, while I might be up for a game of ping pong during lunch, when it comes to hitting deadlines, I'm as firm as a librarian shushing a rowdy reader. And trust me, finding that balance is a skill worth mastering; just ask my team ... once they finish their game.

- **Time Management:** Transitioning into a managerial role often means juggling multiple tasks and priorities. Prioritize your responsibilities, delegate effectively, and don't hesitate to seek support from your own manager or mentor.

Ah, transitioning into a managerial role, where the land of multitasking stretches as far as the eye can see! It's like being handed a plate of spaghetti and being told, "Make it into a gourmet meal." So, here's how I navigate this spaghetti bowl of responsibilities:

First off, prioritizing is key. Just like picking out the juiciest meatball from the spaghetti, I focus on the tasks that are most critical and time-sensitive. If it's not crucial, it can simmer on the back burner for a bit. Now, delegation is an art form. It's like having sous chefs in the kitchen—you need to trust them to chop those onions while you're off flambeing the dessert. Assign tasks to the right people, play to their strengths, and watch the magic happen. And let's not forget about seeking support. It's like calling for backup when the kitchen's on fire; you need help, and there's no shame in asking for it. Whether it's leaning on my own manager for guidance or tapping into the wisdom of a seasoned mentor, I'm not afraid to admit when I need a lifeline.

Now, if you're looking for a detailed education on time management, well, that's a whole other cookbook. But for now, let's just stick to mastering the art of spaghetti juggling with a side of humor, shall we?

I once found myself buried under a mountain of paperwork, drowning in emails, and struggling to keep up with team meetings. Feeling overwhelmed, I reached out to a seasoned manager for advice. Their simple yet profound suggestion? "Focus on what truly matters and let go of the rest." It was a lesson in prioritization that has stayed with me ever since.

Below, I've whipped up a delightful concoction of tips to transform you from a mere mortal into a magnificent first-time manager. So, grab your cape and get ready to conquer those challenges with style!

Useful Tips

- **Invest in Continuous Learning:** Take advantage of training programs, workshops, and resources offered by your organization to hone your managerial skills. Additionally, seek out books, podcasts, and online courses on leadership and team management to expand your knowledge base.

Ah, the realm of continuous learning, where the wise don their metaphorical wizard hats and embark on quests for knowledge! As a manager, I've come to realize that sharpening my skills is not just a noble pursuit, but a necessary one in the ever-changing landscape of leadership. So, picture me donning my invisible cape of curiosity, ready to conquer the daunting peaks of managerial mastery.

> ➢ **Embrace the Resources at Your Workplace:** Think of your organization's training programs and workshops as your own personal Hogwarts. Sure, there might not be any flying broomsticks, but mastering conflict resolution can sometimes feel like battling a horde of dementors. Plus, who doesn't love free coffee and stale pastries?

- ➢ **Explore Beyond the Castle Walls:** Don't limit yourself to just what your workplace offers. Venture into the enchanted forest of self-improvement with books, podcasts, and online courses. It's like embarking on a quest for knowledge, except you don't have to worry about encountering any trolls (unless you count internet trolls).
- ➢ **Listen to the Wise Elders:** Podcasts are like having a council of wise elders at your fingertips, ready to share their insights on leadership and team management. It's like attending a masterclass without having to leave the comfort of your own hobbit hole.
- ➢ **Level Up with Online Courses:** Online courses offer the flexibility to learn at your own pace, which is perfect for busy managers. Plus, the satisfaction of earning digital badges and certificates is almost as rewarding as defeating a particularly challenging boss in a video game (almost).
- ➢ **Keep the Adventure Alive:** Approach continuous learning with a curious spirit and a sprinkle of humor. Treat it like the grand adventure that it is, complete with dragons to slay and treasures to uncover. After all, who said learning can't be fun?

- **Communicate Openly and Transparently:** Foster a culture of open communication within your team where everyone feels comfortable sharing ideas, concerns, and feedback. Be transparent about organizational changes, goals, and expectations to build trust and alignment. Imagine you're the captain of a quirky spaceship crew, hurtling through the vast expanse of the galaxy. Your mission? To explore strange new worlds, seek out new life and civilizations, and boldly go where no one has gone before. But to navigate the cosmic chaos, you need your crew firing on all cylinders, always communicating openly and transparently.

First off, make sure your comms channels are as open as the vacuum of space itself. Encourage everyone onboard to speak up, whether they've discovered a new alien species or just think the coffee in the mess hall could use an upgrade. No idea is too outlandish or irrelevant when you're charting the unknown. And when it comes to sharing news and updates, don't leave your crew in the dark. Be transparent about any changes to the mission plan, whether it's a detour to investigate a mysterious anomaly or just a shift in the onboard movie night schedule. Keeping everyone in the loop builds trust faster than you can say "warp speed."

Remember, in the vast expanse of the cosmos (or the office), a culture of open communication is your best tool for steering clear of black holes and navigating the stars together. So, set phasers to "transparent," engage the warp drive of openness, and boldly communicate like no team has communicated before!

- **Lead by Example:** Your actions speak louder than words. Model the behaviors and work ethic you want to see in your team members. Whether it's staying organized, demonstrating resilience in the face of challenges, or showing empathy toward colleagues, lead by example to inspire your team. Let's imagine you're the leader of a team in a bustling office environment. Leading by example means embodying the traits and behaviors you want to see in your team members. Let's break it down:

- **Staying Organized:** Picture this: your desk resembles the aftermath of a paper tornado. Papers everywhere, sticky notes clinging for dear life to your monitor, and pens mysteriously disappearing into the abyss. Now, that's not the vibe you want to set. Instead, lead by example by keeping your workspace tidy and organized. Show them how it's done—maybe even throw in a label maker for good measure. Your team will appreciate the clarity and efficiency that comes with a clutter-free environment.
- **Demonstrating Resilience:** When faced with challenges, it's important to show your team not just what not to do, but also what a resilient response looks like. For example, imagine a critical system goes down just before a major client presentation. A poor response might involve panicking, assigning blame, or freezing under pressure. A resilient leader, on the other hand, remains calm, communicates transparently, quickly delegates tasks to troubleshoot the issue, and offers a backup plan to the client. This not only keeps things on track but also models composure and problem-solving under pressure—qualities that inspire confidence and trust.
- **Showing Empathy Toward Colleagues:** We've all been there—the dreaded double-booked meeting dilemma. Instead of pointing fingers or playing the blame game, approach the situation with empathy and understanding. Maybe even share a personal anecdote about your own scheduling mishaps to lighten the mood. By showing genuine concern for your colleagues' well-being and workload, you foster a supportive atmosphere where teamwork thrives.

Remember, leading by example isn't just about talking the talk—it's about walking the walk (preferably without tripping over your own feet). So, whether you're organizing your workspace, facing challenges with resilience, or showing empathy toward your team, let your actions do the talking. Who knows, you might just inspire your colleagues to follow suit—tidy desk labels and all.

- **Delegate Wisely:** Delegation is key to effective team management, but it requires trust and clear communication. Delegate tasks based on each team member's strengths, interests, and development goals. Provide guidance and support when needed, but also empower your team to take ownership of their responsibilities.

Let's talk about the art of delegation, shall we? Picture this, you're the captain of a ship navigating through the stormy seas of project management. Now, you might be tempted to hoist all the sails yourself and steer the ship single-handedly, but trust me, that's a recipe for disaster. Instead, delegate tasks like a seasoned captain, ensuring the ship sails smoothly toward success. First things first, know your crew. Each member brings their own unique set of skills, interests, and aspirations to the table. It's like having a treasure chest full of diverse talents waiting to be unleashed. So, when delegating tasks, be like a wise pirate divvying up the booty—match each task with the right crew member's strengths and passions.

For instance, if you've got a crewmate who's a whiz with numbers and loves crunching data like it's a treasure map, why not entrust them with managing the financial aspects of your project? Not only does this play to their strengths, but it also keeps them engaged and motivated; after all, who doesn't love counting gold coins?

But remember, delegation isn't just about handing off tasks and washing your hands of the matter. No, no, it's more like being a mentor guiding your crew through uncharted waters. Provide clear instructions, offer support when needed, and be there to navigate them through rough patches. And here's the kicker—empower your crew to take ownership of their responsibilities. Give them the freedom to make decisions, to explore new horizons, and to boldly go where no crew member has gone before. After all, a crew that feels trusted and valued is a crew that will go to the ends of the earth (or, in this case, the project) to ensure success.

So, my dear captain, remember, delegate wisely, communicate clearly, and empower your crew to conquer the high seas of project management.

- **Provide Regular Feedback:** Offer constructive feedback to your team members on a regular basis. Recognize their achievements, provide guidance for improvement, and address any performance issues promptly. Remember to balance praise with constructive criticism to foster growth and development. As the captain of a ship, you are navigating through the stormy seas of productivity and performance. Your crew relies on your guidance to steer them in the right direction. Here's how you can provide regular feedback to your team members.
  - **Set Sail with Recognition:** Start by recognizing the bright spots in your team's journey. Maybe someone hit a milestone, completed a project ahead of schedule, or brewed the perfect

pot of coffee for the morning meetings (because let's face it, caffeine is the real MVP). Acknowledge these achievements with a hearty "Ahoy, matey! Well done on navigating those choppy waters and finding the treasure!"

- **Course Correction with Guidance:** Now, onto the not-so-smooth sailing parts. If someone's heading off course, gently guide them back with a nudge in the right direction. Remember, it's all about constructive criticism, not walking the plank. Maybe someone's been spending a bit too much time chatting with the office parrot instead of hitting their targets. You could say, "Ahoy there! Let's steer our ship back on course and focus those sea-faring skills on our tasks. The parrot can wait for its moment in the spotlight later!"
- **Tackling Troublesome Waters:** Addressing performance issues is like plugging leaks in the hull before the ship goes down. Don't let problems fester like a forgotten sandwich in the break room fridge. Tackle them head-on but with finesse. For instance, if someone's been consistently missing deadlines, you might say, "Avast ye! We need to tighten our sails and ensure we're hitting those deadlines like cannonballs hitting their mark. Let's work together to patch up any leaks in our time management ship."

Remember, striking the right balance between praise and constructive criticism is key to keeping your crew motivated and sailing smoothly toward success.

- **Build Relationships:** Take the time to get to know your team members on a personal level. Understanding their motivations, aspirations, and communication preferences will help you build stronger relationships and effectively support their growth and development.

So, if you want to take your team to the next level, think of yourself as the Sherlock Holmes of team dynamics, but with a bit more empathy and fewer deerstalkers.

Picture this: You stroll into the office kitchen for your morning coffee, and instead of robotically grabbing your cup and heading back to your desk, you engage in a little friendly banter with your team members. Maybe you discover that Sarah, from accounting, dreams of opening her own bakery one day, or that John, from marketing, is secretly training for a marathon. These little nuggets of personal information aren't just idle gossip—they're golden opportunities to connect on a deeper level. Understanding what makes your team members tick isn't about being nosy (though a touch of nosiness can't hurt), it's about conveying that you know and appreciate their other interests or concerns. Your interest and empathy create mutual trust with the team members that are the building blocks of a strong relationship. After all, knowing that Tina prefers emails over face-to-face chats or that David thrives on public recognition can make all the difference when it comes to fostering a productive and harmonious team dynamic. And who knows, you might even uncover some hidden talents or shared interests along the way.

- **Stay Flexible and Adapt:** The business landscape is constantly evolving, and as a manager, you need to stay agile and adaptable. Be open to new ideas, embrace change, and be willing to adjust your strategies as needed to navigate challenges and seize opportunities.

Alright, imagine you're the head chef in a bustling kitchen, cooking up a storm (pun intended) amidst the chaos of the dinner rush. You've got your recipes, your ingredients, and your trusty spatula ready. But, as any seasoned chef knows, the kitchen can be a hotbed of surprises. Sometimes you run out of key ingredients, the oven decides to play hide-and-seek with your soufflé, or a rogue customer requests a vegan version of your famous steak.

Now, picture this, you've meticulously planned your menu for the evening, but suddenly, your main ingredient is nowhere to be found. Do you stubbornly stick to your original plan, hoping the missing ingredient magically appears? Or do you whip up a creative alternative, transforming a potential disaster into a culinary masterpiece? Well, as a culinary maestro and a wise manager, you opt for the latter. You understand that in the fast-paced world of the kitchen, flexibility is your secret sauce. You can't control every ingredient, but you can control how you adapt to the situation. So, you rally your sous chefs, brainstorm innovative substitutions, and turn adversity into opportunity. Maybe you create a brand-new dish that becomes the talk of the town, or perhaps you impress your diners with your quick thinking and improvisational skills.

So, embrace the chaos of the kitchen, and remember that even when things don't go according to plan, you have the skills and creativity to whip up something amazing. Bon appétit!

- **Prioritize Well-Being:** Don't forget to prioritize your own well-being along with that of your team. Practice self-care, set boundaries, and encourage a healthy work-life balance among your team members. Remember, a happy and healthy team is a more engaged and productive team.

Imagine you're the conductor of your own symphony, orchestrating the harmony of work and well-being. But here's the kicker—you're not just waving the baton for the musicians; you're also playing your own instrument in the band. So, let's fine-tune this composition without missing a beat or getting drowned out in the noise.

First off, self-care isn't just a fleeting melody; it's the bassline that keeps the rhythm steady. Think of yourself as a DJ spinning tunes at a party. You can't keep the crowd moving if you're running on empty. Take a pause, adjust your headphones, and groove to your own tempo. You'll find that the crowd follows suit. Setting boundaries is like marking your territory on a map without building a fortress. Picture yourself as an explorer trekking through uncharted terrain. If the path gets too rocky or the jungle too dense, it's okay to pitch a tent and rest. Let your team know that there are off-limit zones beyond certain hours. The journey can wait until dawn.

Encouraging a healthy work-life balance is akin to crafting a signature cocktail. You need the right mix of ingredients: work, yes, but also a splash of leisure, a twist of family time, and a garnish of personal pursuits. Shake it up with finesse, and serve it with a smile. It's about savoring each sip without getting too tipsy.

And remember, a contented team is like a symphony in perfect harmony. Lead the ensemble with flair. Show them that it's alright to pause for a solo, to share a laugh during intermission, or to applaud each other's achievements. After all, we're all part of the same orchestra, playing our hearts out in this grand performance called life.

By incorporating these tips into your managerial approach, you'll be better equipped to overcome the initial challenges of transitioning from salesperson to first-time manager and lead your team to success. Transitioning from salesperson to first-time manager is a challenging yet rewarding journey. Embrace the learning opportunities, lean on your past experiences, and don't be afraid to ask for help along the way.

Best of luck with your managerial adventure! "Success is not final, failure is not fatal: It is the courage to continue that counts."—Winston Churchill

10

GUIDING THE GUIDERS

"Leadership is not about being in charge. It's about taking care of those in your charge."

–Simon Sinek

Now, picture yourself not just as the captain of a rowing team, but as the coach overseeing multiple boats. Each boat has its own captain, and your job is to make sure those captains are guiding their crews in sync—all rowing in the same direction, with coordinated rhythms, and without veering off course. It's about building cohesion not just within teams, but across teams. And yes, there will be days when it feels less like leadership and more like refereeing a chaotic regatta. But this is the real challenge—and the real reward—of being a manager of managers: steering not just one team, but an entire fleet.

From Player to Coach: The Transition

So, you've just stepped into the world of management, huh? Before you start off, let me share some wisdom. As a fledgling manager, your main gig is to figure out your own style of leadership. It's a bit like trying on different hats to see which one fits best. Are you the laid-back, supportive type, or more of a take-charge, no-nonsense leader? Maybe you're somewhere in between.

Now, picture yourself as the captain of a rowing team. You've got a bunch of folks in the boat, each rowing to their own rhythm. Your job? To get everyone synchronized, rowing in the same direction without crashing into each other. It's all about building that cohesive team spirit, like a well-oiled machine. And trust me, there will be days when you feel more like a referee at a chaotic sports match than a manager. But hold onto your hat, because if you think that's a wild ride, just wait until you level up to becoming a manager's manager. And then, you move up a notch to running the tournament involving multiple teams! You've got to think strategically, anticipate your opponents' moves, and make sure every player on your team is in the right place at the right time. It's like juggling flaming torches while riding a unicycle—exhilarating, but also a tad terrifying.

Delegation becomes your best friend. You can't micromanage every little move anymore; you've got bigger fish to fry. So, you learn to trust your team, pass on tasks like a hot potato, and hope they don't drop it (or worse, toss it back at you).

Conflict resolution? Oh boy, get ready to play mediator, therapist, and sometimes referee all rolled into one. You're the peacekeeper in a world of office politics and personality clashes. It's like being the Gandalf of the workplace—you shall not pass ... without sorting out your issues first! But hey, don't let the pressure get to you. With great power comes great ... well, you know the rest. Just remember to stay humble, keep learning, and never underestimate the importance of a good sense of humor. After all, laughter is the best stress reliever, especially when you're juggling flaming torches on a unicycle!

Remember when you were a first-time manager, basking in the glow of newfound responsibility? Ah, those were the days of directly influencing the team, troubleshooting daily hurdles, and celebrating victories firsthand. But now, as a manager's manager, it's less about scoring goals yourself and more about coaching others to score.

Imagine you're overseeing two managers, Alice and Bob. Alice is struggling with team motivation, while Bob's team consistently misses deadlines. As a manager's manager, your role is to provide guidance and support to help them improve. You might coach Alice on effective motivational techniques and work with Bob to refine his team's project management strategies.

Managing managers comes with its own set of complexities. You're no longer just responsible for your team's performance; you're also accountable for the success of the managers under your wing. This means balancing individual coaching with team cohesion, navigating interdepartmental politics, and fostering a culture of collaboration among your management cohort.

Alrighty, buckle up for a rollercoaster of situations and nifty tips to skyrocket your success!

- **Communicate Clearly and Frequently:** Transparency is key when managing managers. Keep everyone informed about overarching goals, expectations, and any changes in direction.

First things first, be as clear as a freshly Windexed window about your goals. No one likes playing a game without knowing the rules, right? So, lay it all out.

Next up, expectations. Think of these like the guardrails on a roller coaster—you need them to keep things on track and prevent anyone from flying off into the unknown. Spell out what you expect from each manager, but remember, it's a two-way street. Encourage them to share their expectations too, just to keep things fair and square.

Now, changes in direction. Life's full of surprises, isn't it? Like when you're driving and suddenly Google Maps decides you need a scenic detour. When things change, don't keep it a secret like it's a surprise birthday party. Let your managers know ASAP. They might grumble a bit, but hey, at least they won't feel like they've been blindfolded and spun around like pinatas at a birthday bash.

So, in a nutshell, be a transparent maestro, not a mysterious magician. Your managers will thank you, and who knows, maybe they'll even give you a standing ovation (or at least a high-five in the break room).

- **Trust, But Verify:** Delegate responsibilities to your managers, but don't forget to follow up. Trust, but verify progress and offer support where needed.

It's like lending your friend your favorite book and then sneakily checking if they've actually read it before launching into a deep discussion about the plot twists. So, dear reader, here's the deal, when you delegate responsibilities to your trusty managers, it's like sending them off on a quest armed with your trusty sword... or spreadsheet, whichever suits your managerial style. Now, imagine you've entrusted your diligent manager, let's call them Susan, with the task of conquering the dragon of quarterly reports. You've got faith in Susan's ability to slay spreadsheets like a pro, but hey, even the mightiest dragon slayers can stumble. So, it's time to put on your detective hat (metaphorically speaking, unless you're really into cosplay at work) and verify how Susan's doing. Maybe she's battling Excel formulas like a champ, or perhaps she's gotten lost in the labyrinth of pivot tables.

But fear not! Your follow-up isn't about breathing down Susan's neck like an overbearing boss. It's about offering support, like Gandalf appearing at just the right moment with sage advice and a well-timed magical spell. So, check in with Susan, see how she's faring, and if need be, swoop in with guidance or resources to help her vanquish those pesky spreadsheets.

Remember, trust is crucial, but a little verification never hurt anyone. After all, even Frodo had Samwise Gamgee by his side to double-check the map to Mount Doom. Trust Susan to slay the dragons, but don't forget to peek over her shoulder occasionally to make sure she's not accidentally wandering into the lair of the quarterly budget beast.

- **Develop Leadership Skills:** Encourage your managers to grow as leaders themselves. Provide opportunities for training, mentorship, and skill development.

First off, let's talk about training. You know, that thing you send your managers to so they can learn how to be even more awesome? Yeah, that's the ticket. Think about workshops, seminars, or even online courses that can beef up their skills. Maybe they need a crash course in conflict resolution or a masterclass in time management. Whatever it is, just make sure it's as engaging as a Netflix binge session.

Now, onto mentorship: your manager has paired up with seasoned pros who can show them the ropes, share war stories, and drop nuggets of wisdom like confetti at a party. Mentorship is like having a personal Yoda guiding you through the galaxy of leadership. So, find those wise Jedi masters within your organization and let them work their magic. Last but not least, skill development. It's like the gym for your brain. You wouldn't expect to bench press 300 pounds without hitting the weights, right? Same goes for leadership. Give your managers opportunities to stretch their muscles, whether it's by taking on new projects, leading teams, or even trying their hand at public speaking. Who knows, they might even discover hidden talents they never knew they had.

So, there you have it, my friend. Train, mentor, develop—the trifecta of leadership greatness. With a little bit of effort and a whole lot of encouragement, you'll have a team of leaders ready to conquer the world. Now go forth and unleash the power of awesome leadership!

Ah, how could I forget the pièce de resistance? Nestled within the pages of this magnificent book, I've carved out a special spot just for leadership. It's like finding a golden ticket in a chocolate bar, only better because it's filled with wisdom instead of sugar (though a little sugar never hurt anyone). So yes, my dear reader, fear not! I've thought ahead and included a whole chapter dedicated to the art and science of leadership. Consider it your secret weapon, your roadmap to greatness, your very own treasure map leading straight to the land of effective leadership. So, as you dive into the depths of this book, remember to keep an eye out for that shiny chapter on leadership. It's like the cherry on top of an already delicious sundae. And who knows, maybe it'll be the catalyst that propels you and your managers to leadership stardom.

- **Promote Collaboration:** Foster a culture of teamwork among your management team. Encourage knowledge sharing, cross-departmental collaboration, and peer support.

Let's delve into the world of fostering collaboration within your management team, shall we? Picture that you're the captain of a mighty ship, navigating through the choppy seas of corporate waters. Now, you could try to steer that ship all by yourself, but trust me, you'll end up going in circles faster than a confused seagull. Instead, what you need is a crew that works together like a well-oiled machine. Start by setting the tone from the top down. Encourage your management team to share their knowledge freely, like a potluck dinner where everyone brings their best dish to the table. Whether it's a new strategy, a fresh perspective, or just some killer Excel shortcuts, sharing is caring, folks!

But wait, there's more! Break down those departmental barriers like a wrecking ball through a flimsy cubicle wall. Encourage cross-departmental collaboration so that your marketing wizards can brainstorm with your finance gurus, and your HR mavens can join forces with your tech geniuses. Who knows, they might just come up with the next big thing while arguing over who makes the best coffee. And let's not forget about peer support. We're all in this together, folks! Encourage your team to lift each other up like a group of cheerleaders at a high school pep rally. Whether it's offering a helping hand, lending an empathetic ear, or just sharing a well-timed meme to lighten the mood, supporting each other is what teamwork is all about.

So, there you have it, my fellow captain of industry. Foster that culture of teamwork, encourage knowledge sharing, break down those departmental silos, and support each other like there's no tomorrow. And who knows, with a little collaboration magic, you might just steer your ship straight into the sunset of success. Smooth sailing, my friend!

- **Lead by Example:** Your managers will look to you for guidance and inspiration. Model the behavior and values you want to see reflected in your team.

Leading by example is crucial for any leader. After all, if you expect your team to follow certain behaviors and values, you need to show them how it's done. Your crew will take cues from your actions more than your words. Imagine you're in a workplace where punctuality is key. You can't expect your team to arrive on time if you're constantly strolling in fifteen minutes late with a coffee in hand and a sheepish grin. Instead, be the first one at the office, bright-eyed and ready to tackle the day. Your team will notice, and they'll be more inclined to follow suit.

Let's talk about communication. If you want open and transparent communication within your team, you can't be holed up in your office, only emerging to bark orders or send cryptic emails. Be approachable. Have those casual conversations in the break room. Answer questions honestly. Show your team that it's okay to speak up and share their ideas.

And speaking of ideas, don't be afraid to get your hands dirty. If you're leading a project, don't just delegate tasks and disappear into the background. Jump in, roll up your sleeves, and work alongside your team. Not only does this show that you're willing to put in the effort, but it also builds camaraderie and trust. Imagine you're trying to encourage a healthier lifestyle in the workplace. Instead of sending out a dry memo about the benefits of eating salad, why not lead a lunchtime yoga session or challenge your team to a fruit-eating contest? In essence, leading by example is about being the person you want your team to be. So, whether it's showing up on time, fostering open communication, or promoting healthy habits, remember, you're not just the leader, you're the role model.

Empowering Your Team to Make Decisions

The art of decision making comes from making decisions. One has to empower teams to take decisions, keeping the clear objective in mind. There could be some decisions that do not go our way; however, the teams must not be reprimanded on the same, instead have joint discussions to learn from what has happened and understand what should have been done for a positive outcome. Once your teams are habituated to take calls, keeping the end objective and the bigger picture in mind, it soon becomes a way of life and that's when organizations grow, thrive, and prosper.

Picture yourself as the captain of a ship navigating through the unpredictable waters of business. Your crew, your team, they're your ultimate navigators, but you can't be the one holding the compass at every turn. No sir, that would just leave you with cramped hands and a very cranky crew. So, what's the secret sauce here? Empowerment, my friend. You've got to trust your crew to hoist the sails and adjust the rudder while keeping their eyes on the prize—that glorious treasure island of success. Sure, sometimes they might steer you into a storm, but hey, isn't that how epic tales are born?

Now, when things go awry, and they will, resist the urge to play the blame game. Instead, gather around the proverbial campfire and hash it out. What went wrong? What could we have done differently? And most importantly, what can we learn from this adventure? Think of it like this, your team is a bunch of mini Captain Jack Sparrows, savvy and daring, ready to take on the seven seas of business. And you, well, you're more like their wise old parrot, squawking words of wisdom from your perch. Together, you'll navigate through the treacherous waters, uncovering hidden treasures, and avoiding the occasional shipwreck.

So, loosen those reins, let your crew spread their wings, and watch as your ship sails to newfound horizons. After all, in the game of business, it's not just about making decisions, it's about empowering your team to make the right ones. And when you do, oh, the adventures you'll have!

Ascending to the role of a manager's manager is a testament to your leadership skills and potential. Embrace the challenges, learn from your experiences, and never stop striving for excellence. By empowering and supporting your managers, you'll not only drive success within your teams but also leave a lasting impact on the organization as a whole. Remember, humor is often found in the everyday challenges of management. Keep a light heart, stay adaptable, and enjoy the journey ahead!

I once helped a man climb a mountain and found that I too had reached the top.

11

NAVIGATING THE LEADERSHIP MAZE—HARMONIZING LEADERSHIP

In the labyrinth of modern business dynamics, where hierarchies blur and teamwork reigns supreme, the role of leadership emerges as both a beacon and a puzzle. As we embark on this chapter journeying through the intricacies of managing managers and fostering flourishing sales teams, it becomes evident that leadership isn't merely about wielding authority; it's about orchestrating harmony within the ensemble.

Ah, the curious case of leadership, a realm where egos often inflate faster than a hot air balloon at a carnival. Picture this: I'm at the helm of a team, riding the wave of success like a pro surfer on a sunny day. Oh, the joy! The accolades shower down, and naturally, I'm soaking it all in. "Yes, yes, it's all thanks to my brilliant leadership," I might be tempted to think, as my ego inflates faster than a helium balloon at a birthday party. But alas, life is not always a beach holiday. Suddenly, the tide turns, and our ship hits rough waters. Mistakes are made, deadlines missed, and blame starts ricocheting faster than a pinball in a frenzy. Now, some leaders might find themselves playing a game of hot potato with accountability, tossing it to anyone but themselves. "It's not my fault!" they cry as they point fingers faster than a kid caught with their hand in the cookie jar.

But wait, what's this? A true leader emerges from the chaos like a lighthouse in a storm. They don't run from accountability; oh no, they embrace it like a long-lost friend. "Yes, we stumped," they declare, "but together, we'll rise stronger." And when the sun shines again, they don't hoard the spotlight like a greedy magpie with shiny trinkets. No, they shine it on their team, basking in their success like a proud parent at a school play.

Picture this: a team so seamlessly united that the lines between leader and follower fade into obscurity. They move with synchronicity, each member empowered to take charge when the melody of opportunity arises. This, my friends, is the essence of leadership—building a team so strong that they don't recognize a single figure as the definitive leader. Instead, they see themselves as equals on a quest for collective success. But beware the pitfalls of ineffective leadership! An inept captain of the ship often mistakes responsibility for power and privilege, steering the vessel toward treacherous waters. In such scenarios, chaos ensues, and the once-promising journey morphs into a tempest of discontent and disarray. A leader who fails to understand that responsibility is a mantle, not a pedestal, risks alienating the very crew they aim to guide. But how does one avoid the pitfalls of glory-hogging and blame-shifting, you might ask? Well, dear reader, the path to becoming a better leader is paved with self-awareness and humility. Take a long, hard look in the mirror and ask yourself: Am I leading for the greater good, or just to stroke my own ego? Learn to listen, really listen, to the voices of those you lead. And when the chips are down, don't hide behind excuses; stand tall, take responsibility, and watch as respect blooms like a flower in the spring.

Allow me to regale you with a tale, for what better way to illuminate the essence of leadership than through narrative? Imagine a bustling sales floor, alive with the hum of ambition and the buzz of transactions. At its helm stands a leader, not as a figurehead perched upon a pedestal of authority, but as a humble facilitator of greatness. This leader, let's call her Emily, understands that her role isn't to command, but to empower. She fosters an environment where each salesperson feels valued, where ideas are welcomed with open arms, and where success is a shared triumph.

One day, amidst the flurry of activity, an unexpected challenge arises—a key client threatens to walk away. Panic flirts with the edges of the team's composure, but Emily remains unruffled. Instead of barking orders, she gathers her team and invites them to brainstorm solutions. In this moment, the distinction between leader and team dissolves, leaving only a collective resolve to tackle the obstacle head-on. Through collaboration and creativity, they devise a strategy that not only salvages the client relationship but strengthens it. As they celebrate their victory, it becomes clear—Emily isn't just a leader; she's the invisible thread stitching together the fabric of their success.

Dear reader, as we delve deeper into the realms of leadership in the following pages, let us remember the words of wisdom woven into our narrative. Let us strive not for dominance, but for unity. Let us lead not with a heavy hand, but with a guiding light that illuminates the path to greatness for all. For in the dance of leadership, it is not the steps we take but the harmony we create that truly defines our journey.

Remember, dear leaders, power and privilege are but fleeting illusions. True greatness lies not in the accolades you amass, but in the hearts you touch and the lives you uplift. So, lead with integrity, lead with empathy, and above all, lead with humility. And who knows? Maybe one day, they'll write songs about your leadership prowess. Or at the very least, they'll name a sandwich after you in the office cafeteria.

Ah, the intricate dance of leadership—a waltz between art and science, a delicate balance between guiding and inspiring. As we embark on this journey through the labyrinth of leadership, allow me to be your navigator, your guide through the choppy waters and sunlit shores of effective leadership.

Let's start with the basics. Picture yourself at the helm of a ship, navigating through the stormy seas of business challenges. Now, imagine you're not just a captain, but a maestro conducting an orchestra of talent. Your role isn't just to steer the ship; it's to harmonize the efforts of your team, to empower them to reach their full potential. Take Emily, for example, the epitome of leadership finesse. She doesn't just lead; she orchestrates greatness. When faced with adversity, she doesn't bark orders; she invites collaboration. And when success blooms, she doesn't hog the spotlight; she shines it on her team like a proud parent.

Leadership is indeed a multifaceted concept, often described as a delicate dance between art and science. Let's break down this metaphorical waltz.

Art

Leadership is an art form because it involves creativity, intuition, and emotional intelligence. Like an artist painting on a canvas, a leader must have the vision to see the big picture and the ability to inspire others to contribute to it. This artistic element comes into play when leaders must make decisions that aren't solely based on data or logic but require an understanding of human dynamics, motivation, and psychology.

Picture this: I'm the maestro of a bustling workplace symphony, conducting my team with the finesse of a seasoned artist. Leading isn't just about crunching numbers; it's an intricate dance of creativity, intuition, and emotional finesse. Imagine I'm faced with a project that's as messy as a Jackson Pollock painting. There's data to analyze, sure, but there's also the delicate brushstrokes of human interaction to consider. Do I simply go with the cold, hard facts, or do I tap into my emotional intelligence to understand what truly motivates my team?

It's like trying to wrangle a group of cats into a synchronized swimming routine. Sure, I could bark orders and expect them to fall in line, but where's the artistry in that? Instead, I use my intuition to coax out their strengths, inspiring them to contribute their own colorful strokes to the canvas of our project. Like a painter stepping back to admire their masterpiece, I take a moment to appreciate the harmony we've created together. It's not just about reaching the end goal; it's about the journey we take to get there, guided by the subtle nuances of leadership artistry. And hey, if a few paint spills and cat-herding mishaps happen along the way, that just adds to the charm, doesn't it?

Mastering the art of leadership is akin to honing any craft—it takes dedication, practice, and a willingness to learn from both successes and failures. Here's a breakdown of how one can embark on this journey:

- **Study the Masters:** Just as an aspiring painter studies the works of renowned artists, aspiring leaders should delve into the teachings and practices of great leaders past and present. This includes reading books, attending workshops, and seeking mentorship from experienced leaders.
- **Embrace Creativity:** Like an artist exploring new techniques and styles, a leader should foster a creative mindset. This involves thinking outside the box, encouraging innovation, and being open to unconventional ideas.
- **Develop Intuition:** Much like an artist's instinct guides their brushstrokes, a leader's intuition guides their decision-making process. This means learning to trust your gut feelings while also balancing them with rational analysis.
- **Cultivate Emotional Intelligence:** A crucial aspect of leadership artistry is understanding and empathizing with others. This involves recognizing emotions, managing interpersonal relationships, and effectively communicating with empathy.
- **Practice Self-Reflection:** Just as an artist critiques their own work to improve, leaders should regularly reflect on their actions and behaviors. This helps identify strengths to build upon and areas for growth.
- **Seek Feedback:** Just as an artist welcomes critiques from peers and mentors, leaders should actively seek feedback from

their team members and colleagues. This fosters a culture of continuous improvement and helps identify blind spots.

- **Lead with Authenticity:** Just as each artist has their own unique style, effective leaders embrace their authentic selves. This means leading with integrity, staying true to your values, and building genuine connections with those you lead.
- **Adapt and Evolve:** Like art itself, leadership is fluid and ever-evolving. Successful leaders adapt to changing circumstances, embrace new challenges, and continually refine their skills.

By following these steps and approaching leadership as an art form, one can gradually master the delicate balance of creativity, intuition, and emotional intelligence required to inspire and empower others. And remember, just like a masterpiece, true leadership artistry is never truly finished—it's an ongoing process of growth and refinement.

Science

Leadership also has a scientific aspect to it. This involves the application of theories, models, and empirical evidence to understand human behavior, organizational dynamics, and effective management practices. Just as scientists conduct experiments to test hypotheses, leaders gather data, analyze trends, and adapt their strategies based on evidence and feedback. The science of leadership encompasses fields such as organizational psychology, sociology, and management theory. As a leader, I find the scientific aspect of leadership quite intriguing. It's like conducting a grand experiment where instead of lab rats, you have humans, and instead of test tubes, you have boardrooms. Just as scientists meticulously design experiments to understand the world around them, leaders gather data and insights to navigate the complex terrain of human behavior and organizational dynamics.

Let's take an example from the realm of organizational psychology. Imagine you're leading a team where productivity seems to be dwindling. Instead of resorting to the classic "crack-the-whip" approach, you decide to apply some scientific principles. You gather data on work patterns, employee satisfaction, and team dynamics. Through careful analysis, you discover that certain work processes are causing bottlenecks and demotivating your team members. Armed with this evidence, you implement changes, like restructuring workflows and introducing flexible working hours. Lo and behold, productivity shoots up like a rocket!

This approach not only highlights the importance of empirical evidence in decision-making but also helps you light-heartedly navigate the sometimes-unpredictable world of human behavior. After all, leading a team can often feel like herding cats—except these cats have spreadsheets and deadlines! Mastering the scientific aspect of leadership requires a combination of knowledge, skills, and mindset. Here's a roadmap to help you become a master of this domain:

- **Continuous Learning:** Stay curious and keep expanding your knowledge base. Dive into fields like organizational psychology, sociology, and management theory. Read books, attend seminars, and take courses to deepen your understanding.

- **Apply Theory to Practice:** Don't just absorb theoretical knowledge; actively apply it to real-life situations. Experiment with different leadership strategies and observe their outcomes. Keep a reflective journal to track what works and what doesn't.
- **Embrace Data-Driven Decision-Making:** Cultivate a habit of gathering and analyzing data to inform your decisions. Utilize tools like surveys, performance metrics, and feedback mechanisms to collect relevant information. Make decisions based on evidence rather than gut feelings.
- **Develop Analytical Skills:** Sharpen your analytical skills to interpret data effectively. Learn how to identify patterns, draw insights, and make sound conclusions. This will enable you to spot trends and anticipate challenges before they arise.
- **Foster a Culture of Learning:** Encourage a culture of experimentation and learning within your team or organization. Create safe spaces for people to voice their ideas, try new approaches, and learn from both successes and failures.
- **Seek Feedback and Adapt:** Be open to feedback from colleagues, mentors, and team members. Use feedback as a valuable source of information to refine your leadership approach. Continuously adapt and evolve based on the insights you gain.
- **Lead with Empathy and Humility:** Remember that leadership is ultimately about understanding and inspiring people. Cultivate empathy toward your team members and approach leadership with humility. Acknowledge that you don't have all the answers and be willing to learn from others.

By following these steps and consistently honing your skills, you can master the scientific aspect of leadership. Just remember to approach it with a curious mind, a data-driven mindset, and a healthy dose of humility.

Guiding

Leaders serve as guides, providing direction and clarity amidst uncertainty. Much like a navigator plotting a course through uncharted waters, leaders must chart a path forward for their teams or organizations. This involves setting goals, establishing priorities, and defining strategies to achieve them. Effective leaders communicate their vision effectively, inspiring others to follow their lead and stay committed to the journey ahead.

As a leader, I see myself as a seasoned navigator, equipped with a trusty compass and a map of uncharted waters. My team relies on me to steer us through stormy seas and unknown territories, all the while keeping morale high and spirits afloat. Setting sail on our latest project, I gather my crew together and outline our course. We establish clear goals: reaching the treasure island of Success, navigating past the treacherous whirlpools of Deadline Bay, and avoiding the sirens of Distraction Reef. With priorities set and strategies in mind, we're ready to embark on our adventure. Now, communication is key. I don't just bark orders. Instead, I paint a vivid picture of our destination, describing the shimmering shores of Achievement Beach and the bountiful treasures awaiting us. With my words, I inspire my crew to roll up their sleeves, hoist the sails, and chant our team motto: "Aye Aye, Captain Efficiency!" Of course, along the way, there are bound to be challenges. When we encounter unforeseen obstacles, I don't panic and jump ship like a nervous cabin boy. Instead, I steer us back on course with a mixture of wit and wisdom. "Avast, me hearties!" I'll exclaim, "Let's navigate this rough patch like true buccaneers, with a dash of courage and a sprinkle of creativity!"

And through it all, we press on, united in our mission and fueled by the promise of adventure. Because with me at the helm, leading with guidance, there's no storm we can't weather and no treasure we can't plunder ... I mean, discover!

Mastering the art of guiding as a leader requires a combination of skills, experience, and personal qualities. Here's a breakdown of how one can strive toward mastering this art:

- **Develop Self-Awareness:** Understanding your own strengths, weaknesses, and leadership style is crucial. Reflect on past experiences, gather feedback, and continuously strive for self-improvement.
- **Build Trust:** Trust is the foundation of effective leadership. Be honest, transparent, and reliable in your actions and communications. Show empathy and support for your team members, fostering an environment where everyone feels valued and respected.
- **Communication Skills:** Effective communication is essential for guiding others. Practice active listening, articulate your vision clearly, and tailor your message to resonate with your audience. Use storytelling and humor to engage and inspire your team.
- **Strategic Thinking:** Develop the ability to analyze complex situations, identify opportunities, and formulate strategic

plans. Set clear goals, establish priorities, and adapt your strategies as needed in response to changing circumstances.

- **Decision-Making:** Leaders often face tough decisions. Mastering the art of decision-making involves weighing risks and benefits, consulting with relevant stakeholders, and making timely and informed choices.
- **Inspire and Motivate:** Cultivate a positive and motivational environment where team members feel encouraged to give their best. Lead by example, celebrate successes, and provide constructive feedback to keep morale high and motivation levels up.
- **Adaptability:** In today's fast-paced and unpredictable world, leaders must be adaptable and resilient. Embrace change, learn from failures, and remain flexible in your approach to problem-solving.
- **Lead with Purpose:** Connect your team's work to a larger purpose or vision. Help individuals understand how their contributions fit into the bigger picture, fostering a sense of meaning and fulfillment in their roles.
- **Continuous Learning:** Leadership is a journey of growth and development. Stay curious, seek out new knowledge and experiences, and be open to feedback and constructive criticism.
- **Humility:** Finally, remember that leadership is not about wielding power or seeking personal glory. It's about serving others, empowering your team members to reach their full potential, and achieving collective success.

Mastering the art of guiding as a leader is an ongoing process that requires dedication, practice, and a genuine commitment to the well-being and success of your team. By honing these skills and qualities, you can navigate your team through uncertain waters with confidence and grace.

Inspiring

Inspirational leadership motivates individuals to go above and beyond what they thought possible. Leaders inspire by fostering a sense of purpose, instilling confidence, and empowering others to reach their full potential. Like a beacon of light guiding ships to safety, inspirational leaders illuminate the way forward, even in the darkest of times. They lead by example, embodying the values they espouse and earning the trust and respect of those they lead.

Imagine you're on a stormy sea, surrounded by uncertainty and doubt. In storms like these, people often look for a guiding light, a beacon of hope amidst the chaos. That's where inspirational leadership comes in, and that's where I strive to shine. As a leader, I see myself as that lighthouse, standing tall and unwavering against the crashing waves. My mission isn't just to weather the storm myself but to guide others safely to shore, too. And let's face it, sometimes it feels like herding cats in a hurricane! But how do I do it? Well, first off, I believe in purpose. I'm not just shouting orders from the safety of the shore; I'm out there with my crew, battling the elements, and showing them that there's a reason we're all in this together. It's like convincing a group of penguins to take up synchronized swimming—challenging, but oh so rewarding.

Confidence is key, too. Sure, the waves might be towering over us, but I've got a smile on my face and a twinkle in my eye that says, "We've got this."

Empowerment? Absolutely. I'm not here to micromanage every little detail; I'm here to unleash the hidden talents and potential of each member of my team. It's like being a gardener in a jungle—sometimes you just need to prune a bit here and there to let the real beauty shine. And of course, leading by example is non-negotiable. I'm not asking anyone to do something I wouldn't do myself. If I'm asking them to brave the storm, you better believe I'm out there getting soaked right alongside them. So, there you have it. Inspirational leadership isn't just about talking the talk; it's about strapping on your rain boots, grabbing your umbrella, and dancing through the storm with a smile on your face. And who knows, maybe along the way, you'll inspire a few others to join in the dance too.

Mastering inspirational leadership is a journey rather than a destination, but here are some key steps to help you along the way:

- **Self-Awareness:** Understand your own strengths, weaknesses, values, and motivations. This self-awareness will help you lead authentically and empathetically.
- **Lead by Example:** Actions speak louder than words. Be the embodiment of the qualities you want to inspire in others. Show dedication, integrity, resilience, and humility in your own behavior.
- **Effective Communication:** Develop strong communication skills to convey your vision, values, and goals clearly and

compellingly. Use storytelling and empathy to connect with your team on a personal level.

- **Inspire Purpose:** Help your team members understand the significance of their work and how it contributes to a larger purpose or mission. Encourage them to find meaning and fulfillment in what they do.
- **Build Trust:** Foster an environment of trust and psychological safety where team members feel comfortable taking risks, expressing ideas, and being themselves. Trust is the foundation of strong relationships and effective teamwork.
- **Empower Others:** Delegate responsibility and decision-making authority to your team members, allowing them to take ownership of their work and grow professionally. Provide support and guidance as needed, but allow them the freedom to learn from their experiences.
- **Recognize and Celebrate Achievements:** Acknowledge the efforts and accomplishments of your team members regularly. Celebrate milestones and successes, no matter how small, to boost morale and motivation.
- **Continual Learning and Growth:** Leadership is a lifelong journey of growth and development. Stay curious, seek feedback, and continually strive to improve your leadership skills.
- **Adaptability:** Be flexible and adaptable in your approach to leadership, recognizing that different situations and individuals may require different styles of leadership. Stay open-minded and willing to adjust your approach as needed.
- **Embrace Resilience:** Leadership can be challenging, and setbacks are inevitable. Cultivate resilience by maintaining a

positive attitude, learning from failures, and bouncing back stronger than before.

By consistently practicing these principles and reflecting on your experiences, you can continue to grow and evolve as an inspirational leader. Remember, leadership is not about being perfect but about continuously striving to bring out the best in yourself and others.

Balance

Finding the right balance between guiding and inspiring is key to effective leadership. Too much guidance can stifle creativity and autonomy, while too little can leave followers feeling lost and directionless. Similarly, excessive inspiration without clear direction can lead to aimless enthusiasm, while too much focus on tasks and processes can dampen morale and creativity. Effective leaders strike a balance between providing structure and fostering innovation, offering support while encouraging independence.

Let's put this into a more personal perspective. Finding the sweet spot between being a guiding light and an inspirational force is like trying to balance on a unicycle while juggling flaming torches—it requires finesse and a knack for timing. Picture me as the ringmaster of this leadership circus, if you will. Now imagine I'm leading a team tasked with designing a new product, let's say, a revolutionary coffee mug that can also charge your phone (because who doesn't need that in their life?). If I come in guns blazing with a meticulously detailed plan on exactly how every inch of that mug should be designed, I might inadvertently suffocate the creative sparks of my team. They'll feel like they're just following orders rather than unleashing their inner design wizards. On the flip side, if I swoop in with nothing but rousing speeches about the importance of innovation and thinking outside the box, my team might end up spinning in circles, unsure of where to even start. We'll have a lot of enthusiasm, sure, but it'll be like trying to navigate a ship without a compass—we might end up in uncharted waters.

So, what's a leader to do? Well, it's all about finding that Goldilocks zone—not too hot, not too cold, but just right. I need to provide enough structure to give my team a solid foundation to build upon, like the sturdy handle of our coffee mug, while also leaving enough room for them to sprinkle in their own creative magic, like choosing the perfect color for that mug's sleek design. And hey, sometimes it's okay to throw in a bit of humor to keep spirits high and creativity flowing. Maybe I'll crack a joke about how our coffee mug should also have a built-in alarm clock for those Monday mornings when even caffeine needs a backup plan. Laughter is the secret sauce that keeps the team motivated and the ideas brewing. In the end, effective leadership isn't about being a drill sergeant barking orders or a cheerleader blindly rallying the troops—it's about being that experienced gardener, creating the right conditions for growth, providing support when needed, and knowing when to step back and let the plants thrive on their own. It's a delicate balance, but when done right, the result is nothing short of magical.

Mastering the art of balancing guidance and inspiration in leadership is indeed a journey that requires self-awareness, adaptability, and ongoing learning. Here are some steps you can take to hone this skill:

Know Yourself: Understand your own leadership style, strengths, and weaknesses. Reflect on how you naturally tend to guide and inspire others, and be open to feedback from your team about what they find effective.

Understand Your Team: Get to know your team members individually—their strengths, preferences, and working styles. This understanding will help you tailor your approach to provide the right level of guidance and inspiration for each person.

Set Clear Goals and Expectations: Provide a clear vision and direction for your team, outlining goals and expectations. This gives them a roadmap to follow while still allowing room for creative problem-solving and innovation.

Empower and Delegate: Trust your team members to take ownership of their work and make decisions. Delegate tasks and empower them to find their own solutions, while being available to provide support and guidance when needed.

Communicate Effectively: Maintain open and transparent communication with your team. Clearly communicate goals, provide feedback regularly, and be receptive to input and ideas from others.

Lead by Example: Demonstrate the balance between guidance and inspiration in your own actions and decisions. Show your team what it looks like to provide structure while also fostering creativity and innovation.

Be Flexible and Adaptive: Recognize that the needs of your team may change over time and be willing to adjust your approach accordingly. Stay flexible and adaptive in your leadership style, always seeking to find the right balance for the situation at hand.

Continuously Learn and Improve: Leadership is a journey of growth and development. Stay curious, seek out opportunities for learning and self-improvement, and be willing to experiment with new approaches to leadership.

By consciously practicing these principles and remaining committed to finding the right balance between guidance and inspiration, you can become a more effective and impactful leader for your team. In summary, effective leadership is indeed a complex dance, blending artistry and science, guidance and inspiration. By mastering this intricate waltz, leaders can navigate the challenges of today's dynamic and uncertain world, steering their teams and organizations toward success.

Now, let's talk about the qualities that set leaders like Emily apart from the rest. It's not just about authority; it's about authenticity. A great leader is genuine, transparent, and humble. They listen more than they speak, and when they do speak, it's with empathy and understanding. But here's the kicker—leadership isn't a one-size-fits-all kind of deal. It's a blend of different qualities, a cocktail of skills tailored to your unique strengths and challenges. So, how do you develop these qualities? Well, it starts with self-awareness. Take a long, hard look in the mirror and ask yourself: what kind of leader do I want to be?

Once you've got that figured out, it's time to roll up your sleeves and get to work. Practice active listening, cultivate empathy, and don't be afraid to admit when you're wrong. And above all, lead by example. Be the kind of leader you'd want to follow.

Ah, leadership—that enigmatic blend of charisma, empathy, and a sprinkle of humility. Let's break down what makes leaders like Emily shine brighter than a disco ball at a dance party.

Authenticity

Picture this:
I'm sitting in a team meeting, and our leader, let's call her Emily, is about as genuine as a freshly baked grandma's apple pie. You know the type – no frills, no fluff, just straight-up authenticity. It's like she's allergic to corporate jargon and scripted speeches. So, Emily starts talking, and there's no mistaking it—she's not reading off some teleprompter or regurgitating a rehearsed spiel. Nope, what she says comes straight from the heart, unfiltered and sincere. Take last week, for example. We were discussing a project that hit a few bumps along the way. Instead of trying to spin it into some glossy success story, Emily lays it out like it is. "Well folks," she says with a wry smile, "looks like we hit a bit of a speed bump on this one. But hey, that's life, right? Let's roll up our sleeves and figure this out together."

And you know what? It's refreshing. In a world where everyone's putting on a show, it's nice to have someone like Emily whose no-nonsense approach often comes with a side of subtle humor.

Mastering authenticity, much like perfecting grandma's apple pie recipe, takes time, practice, and a genuine commitment to being true to yourself. Here are some steps to consider:

- **Know Yourself:** Understand your values, beliefs, strengths, and weaknesses. Authenticity starts with self-awareness.
- **Be Honest:** Don't try to be someone you're not or pretend to have qualities you don't possess. Embrace your flaws and imperfections—they're what make you unique.
- **Speak from the Heart:** When you communicate, whether it's in a team meeting or one-on-one conversation, speak sincerely and honestly. Avoid corporate jargon or rehearsed speeches; instead, express yourself genuinely.
- **Listen Actively:** Authenticity isn't just about speaking—it's also about listening. Show genuine interest in others' perspectives and experiences.
- **Be Transparent:** Share your thoughts, feelings, and intentions openly. Transparency builds trust and credibility.
- **Stay Consistent:** Be consistent in your words, actions, and behaviors. Authenticity isn't something you turn on and off—it's a way of being.
- **Embrace Vulnerability:** Being authentic means being willing to show vulnerability. Don't be afraid to admit when you're wrong or ask for help when you need it.
- **Find Your Voice:** Don't be afraid to express your opinions, even if they're unpopular. Authenticity often requires courage to stand up for what you believe in.

- **Practice Empathy:** Understand and empathize with others' perspectives and experiences. Authenticity involves being genuine in your interactions with others.
- **Surround Yourself with Authentic People:** Surround yourself with people who value authenticity and encourage you to be yourself. Authenticity can be contagious in the right environment.

Remember, mastering authenticity is an ongoing journey, not a destination. It's about continually striving to be the most genuine version of yourself in every aspect of your life.

Transparency

This is the art of laying it all out on the table like a buffet spread. A great leader doesn't hide behind closed doors or cloak themselves in mystery. Take Bob, for example. He's like a see-through glass window; you can see right through him (figuratively, of course). He shares information openly, keeps everyone in the loop, and doesn't play hide-and-seek with important updates.

Think of transparency as the ultimate buffet spread—every dish labeled, nothing tucked away in the kitchen. When leaders work this way, trust grows; confusion shrinks; and teams make better, faster decisions because everyone sees the same menu.

Take Bob, for example. He's a figurative glass wall—no curtains, no smoke-and-mirrors. Bob shares project updates before anyone has to ask, admits missteps as soon as they happen, and invites questions instead of dodging them. As a result, his team feels respected, stays aligned, and can course-correct quickly.

Why does this matter?

- **Trust & Credibility:** Openness shows you have nothing to hide, which turns skepticism into confidence.
- **Engagement & Morale:** When people understand the "why" behind decisions, they feel included and motivated.
- **Speed & Agility:** Clear information flows let teams solve problems without stalls or second-guessing.
- **Accountability:** Sunlight reveals both successes and stumbles, making it easier to celebrate wins and address gaps.

In a world already stuffed with secrets, transparent leadership is like handing everyone the answer key to a crossword puzzle: progress accelerates, frustration fades, and the whole group finishes stronger—together.

Humility

Humility—the quiet strength of true leadership. It's not about grandstanding or showing off every achievement like a peacock in full display. It's about staying grounded, approachable, and real.

For example, I like to think of myself as a leader as humble as a slice of plain bread. Nothing flashy—just someone who rolls up their sleeves and works shoulder-to-shoulder with the team.

I remember a time when we were up against a massive project deadline. Instead of standing back and managing from a distance, I jumped right into the thick of it. Picture me with a coffee-stained spreadsheet in hand, fumbling through data like a toddler with a crayon—but doing it with a sense of humor and determination.

That moment wasn't about proving a point. It was about showing my team that we were in it together. And it worked. We didn't just meet the deadline—we did it with a strong sense of camaraderie and shared purpose.

So, while some leaders might prefer to shine in the spotlight, I'll stick with my humble slice of bread. Because in the end, genuine humility builds trust, fosters collaboration, and lights the way forward—no feathers required.

Mastering humility as a leader is no small feat, but it's certainly achievable with the right mindset and approach. Here are some steps one can take to cultivate and master humility:

- **Self-Awareness:** Understand your strengths and weaknesses. Recognize that you don't have all the answers, and that you can learn from others.
- **Listen Actively:** Truly listen to others without interrupting or dismissing their perspectives. Value their input and show genuine interest in what they have to say.
- **Acknowledge Mistakes:** Embrace your imperfections and be willing to admit when you've made a mistake. Apologize sincerely and take steps to rectify the situation.
- **Give Credit Where It's Due:** Acknowledge the contributions of others and celebrate their achievements. Avoid hogging the spotlight, and instead shine it on those who deserve recognition.
- **Stay Grounded:** Remember where you came from and remain humble in the face of success. Don't let accomplishments inflate your ego or disconnect you from your team.

- **Practice Empathy:** Put yourself in others' shoes and consider their perspectives and feelings. Treat everyone with kindness, respect, and compassion.
- **Lead by Example:** Model humility in your actions and interactions with others. Show that humility is not a sign of weakness but rather a strength that fosters trust, collaboration, and growth.
- **Continuously Learn and Grow:** Stay curious and open-minded, always seeking to expand your knowledge and improve yourself. Be willing to learn from everyone around you, regardless of their position or status.
- **Stay Accountable:** Hold yourself accountable for your actions and decisions. Take responsibility for both successes and failures, and use them as opportunities for growth and learning.
- **Maintain Perspective:** Keep in mind that leadership is not about being the center of attention but rather about serving others and achieving common goals together.

By consistently practicing these principles and staying committed to personal growth, one can gradually master humility as a leader and create a positive and empowering environment for their team.

Active Listening

So, what's active listening? It's like tuning in to your favorite radio station, except the frequency is your team's needs and concerns. A top-notch leader like Dave isn't just nodding along like a bobblehead; he's actually absorbing every word like a sponge. He listens, he understands and then he takes action. So let me put on my active listening hat and break it down for you.

So, imagine I'm Dave, your stellar leader, right? Picture me sitting there in a meeting, not just nodding away like one of those dashboard bobbleheads, but fully engaged, soaking up every word like a sponge in a dishwashing commercial. Now, let's say Sally from the marketing team starts talking about this new campaign idea. Instead of zoning out and mentally drafting my grocery list, I'm tuned in. I'm not just hearing her; I'm picking up on the subtle nuances, the hidden gems of insight buried within her words. Maybe she mentions how the target audience responded to a similar campaign last year, or drops a hint about a competitor's weak spot. That's gold! And because I'm actively listening, I catch it. It's like finding that prize-winning ticket at the bottom of a cereal box—unexpected, but oh-so-satisfying.

So, what do I do next? I don't just sit there twiddling my thumbs. Nope, I take action. Maybe I ask Sally to elaborate on those points, or I jot down some notes to explore later. Either way, I'm not just a passive bystander in this conversation; I'm an active participant, ready to turn words into action. And hey, who knows? Maybe by really tuning in and understanding my team's needs and concerns, I'll uncover the next big idea. Or at the very least, I'll earn myself a reputation as the most attentive leader this side of the water cooler. Win-win, right?

Mastering active listening is like honing any skill—it takes practice, patience, and a genuine desire to improve. Here are some steps you can take to become a pro at active listening:

- **Be Present:** Focus on the person speaking and eliminate distractions. Put away your phone, close your laptop, and give them your full attention. Show that you're engaged through non-verbal cues like nodding or maintaining eye contact.
- **Listen Fully:** Instead of just waiting for your turn to speak, genuinely listen to what the other person is saying. Resist the urge to interrupt or finish their sentences. Let them express themselves fully before responding.
- **Paraphrase and Reflect:** After they've finished speaking, paraphrase what they've said to ensure you understand correctly. Reflect on their feelings or concerns to show empathy and understanding. For example, "We can hear your frustration about the delayed project deadlines."
- **Ask Open-Ended Questions:** Encourage the speaker to elaborate by asking open-ended questions. These are questions that can't be answered with a simple yes or no, and they help deepen the conversation and uncover more insights.
- **Practice Empathy:** Put yourself in the speaker's shoes and try to understand their perspective. Validate their feelings and experiences, even if you don't necessarily agree with them. This creates a supportive environment where people feel heard and valued.
- **Stay Neutral:** Avoid jumping to conclusions or making judgments prematurely. Keep an open mind and reserve your opinions until you've heard all sides of the story.
- **Provide Feedback:** Offer constructive feedback when appropriate, but do so in a way that is respectful and considerate. Focus on the issue at hand rather than criticizing the person.

- **Follow Through:** Take action based on what you've heard. Whether it's implementing a new idea, addressing a concern, or offering support, show that you've listened by following through with meaningful actions.

Remember, mastering active listening is an ongoing process. Keep practicing and seeking feedback, and over time, you'll become a skilled listener who can effectively connect with and support others.

Empathy

The secret sauce that turns a good leader into a great one. Picture Jane, the empathy guru. She doesn't just sympathize with her team; she walks a mile in their shoes, feels what they feel, and offers support without hesitation.

Picture this: I'm at the helm; Jane, the empathy extraordinaire. My team isn't just a group of colleagues; they're my companions on this wild journey called work. So, when Tom stumbles in on Monday morning looking like he's been hit by a bus (figuratively speaking, of course), I don't just offer him a sympathetic pat on the back and a "tough break, buddy." No, no, no. Instead, I slip into my metaphorical walking shoes (quite stylish, if I do say so myself) and stride alongside him through the treacherous terrain of last-minute client demands and missed deadlines.

I feel his frustration bubbling like an overcooked pot of spaghetti sauce (which, incidentally, is what I ended up having for dinner last night because, well, life happens). With a knowing nod and a compassionate smile, I offer him the support he needs, like a well-placed cushion for a tired soul. See, empathy isn't just about saying the right words; it's about embodying them, about feeling the rhythm of your team's heartbeat and dancing to its tune. And let me tell you, folks, when you can waltz through the ups and downs of office life with the grace and finesse of a seasoned dancer (or at least with the enthusiasm of someone who's had way too much caffeine), that's when you truly earn your stripes as a leader.

Mastering empathy, like any skill worth having, takes time, practice, and a genuine desire to understand and connect with others on a deeper level. Here's how you can start:

- **Active Listening:** Truly listen to what others are saying without interrupting or thinking about your response. Pay attention to their tone, body language, and emotions behind their words.
- **Put Yourself in Their Shoes:** Imagine yourself in the other person's position. How would you feel if you were experiencing what they're going through? This exercise helps cultivate empathy by allowing you to see things from different perspectives.
- **Ask Open-Ended Questions:** Encourage others to share their thoughts and feelings by asking questions that invite deeper conversation. Avoid yes or no questions, and instead, inquire about their experiences, concerns, and needs.
- **Practice Emotional Awareness:** Tune in to your own emotions and how they may be influencing your interactions with others. By understanding your own feelings, you can better empathize with the emotions of those around you.

- **Validate Emotions:** Acknowledge and validate the emotions of others, even if you don't necessarily agree with them. Let them know that their feelings are heard and respected.
- **Show Genuine Care and Support:** Express genuine care and support for others in both words and actions. Offer assistance when needed and be there to lend a listening ear or a comforting shoulder.
- **Learn from Others:** Observe empathetic individuals in your life, whether they're friends, family members, or colleagues. Take note of their behaviors and communication styles, and incorporate those aspects into your own interactions.
- **Practice Self-Reflection:** Regularly reflect on your interactions with others and evaluate how effectively you're demonstrating empathy. Identify areas for improvement and continue to refine your empathetic skills over time.

Remember, empathy isn't about fixing someone's problems or taking on their emotions as your own. It's about understanding, validating, and supporting others in a way that fosters connection and mutual respect. So, keep practicing, stay open-minded, and always strive to see the world through the eyes of others.

Leading by Example

This means it's like being the trendsetter of the office without even trying. Take Tom, for instance. He doesn't just talk the talk; he walks the walk (and occasionally moonwalks for good measure). Whether it's staying late to meet a deadline or volunteering for the coffee run, he sets the bar high for everyone else to follow. So, picture this: Tom is in the office, just doing his thing, and he realizes something—without even intending to, he's become the trendsetter. Yeah, like the accidental influencer of the workplace. Let's talk about Tom, shall we? This guy doesn't just talk about getting stuff done; he's out there doing it. And when I say doing it, I mean he's walking the walk, and every now and then, he throws in a cheeky moonwalk just for kicks. Classic Tom.

Now, let me give you a little anecdote. There I am, facing a mountain of work, deadlines looming like dark clouds on the horizon. But hey, no sweat, right? Because Tom's here, leading the charge. He's the guy who stays late, not because he has to, but because he's determined to get that project across the finish line. And let's not forget about the coffee run. Tom doesn't just volunteer; he practically sprints to the coffee machine, fueled by caffeine and a sense of duty. So, what's the result of all this Tom-foolery? Well, it's simple. Tom sets the bar sky-high, and the rest of us mere mortals have no choice but to follow suit. I guess you could say he's like our office's unofficial superhero, saving the day one deadline at a time. And as for me? Well, let's just say I'm taking notes, ready to unleash my inner Tom when duty calls. Who knows, maybe one day I'll master the art of the moonwalk too. But until then, I'll just keep watching and learning from the master himself.

The art of mastering the office trendsetter role? Well, it's a delicate balance of charisma, reliability, and a dash of that special something that makes you stand out (maybe not necessarily the moonwalk, but hey, it couldn't hurt!). Here's a breakdown of how you could master it:

Lead by Example: Show, don't tell. Be the first to arrive, the last to leave if needed. Take on tasks with enthusiasm and complete them to the best of your ability. Your actions will speak louder than words.

Build Relationships: Get to know your colleagues. Offer help when needed, and don't be afraid to ask for help when you need it. Being approachable and supportive fosters a positive work environment where people are more inclined to follow your lead.

Stay Positive: Maintain a can-do attitude even when things get tough. Positivity is contagious, and people are naturally drawn to those who exude optimism.

Set Clear Goals: Have a vision for what you want to achieve, both personally and as a team. Communicate these goals clearly and inspire others to join you in pursuing them.

Be Adaptable: Embrace change and be willing to adapt to new situations and challenges. Flexibility is key in a dynamic work environment.

Continuous Learning: Never stop learning and improving yourself. Stay updated with industry trends, acquire new skills, and seek feedback to grow professionally. This gives you the confidence to initiate an action naturally.

Inject Some Fun: A touch of humor and lightheartedness can go a long way in building camaraderie among colleagues. Just like Tom's occasional moonwalk, find ways to inject some fun into the workplace while still getting the job done.

Remember, mastering the role of the office trendsetter is about authenticity and genuine leadership. Stay true to yourself, lead with integrity, and others will naturally be inspired to follow your lead. And who knows, maybe one day you'll have your own cadre of coworkers perfecting their moonwalks alongside you.

Ah, behold the majestic qualities that elevate leaders like myself from the mundane masses. Picture this: authenticity, transparency, humility, active listening, empathy—oh, and let's not forget leading by example. It's like assembling the Avengers of leadership traits, ready to swoop in and rescue the workplace from chaos (or at least spruce it up a bit). First off, authenticity. None of that phony-baloney stuff here—just genuine, unfiltered me. Transparency? My middle name. Well, not really, but you get the idea. Humility? Please, hold your applause. Active listening? I'm all ears ... well, metaphorically speaking. Empathy? I practically ooze it. And leading by example? Let's just say, I'm the Gandalf of the office, leading my fellowship to greatness. In conclusion, as the great Spider-Man once said, "With great power comes great responsibility." And with great leadership traits like these, well, the responsibility to make the workplace awesome falls squarely on my capable shoulders.

Alright, listen up, folks! If you're aiming to be the cream of the leadership crop, it's not about bossing people around like you're the ruler of a tiny empire. No, no, no. It's about being a beacon of inspiration, the kind of leader people actually want to follow. So, here's the deal: ditch the dictator hat and don the mantle of leadership with finesse. You're not just the one barking orders from the top; you're the one who ignites a fire of passion in your team, making them want to give their all. Now, about those pesky micromanagement tendencies. Instead of hovering over your team like a helicopter parent, why not trust them to handle their business? Give them the freedom to spread their wings and watch them soar. Trust me, it's like setting your inner control freak free into the wild!

Oh, and let's talk credit. None of that "I did it all by myself" nonsense. Be the leader who's not afraid to shine the spotlight on your team's brilliance. After all, a pat on the back goes a long way, and you'll earn major brownie points for being the humble hero. Consistency is key, my friends. Think of it like a daily dose of leadership multivitamins. Listen to your team's woes, empower them to tackle challenges head-on, and always keep that integrity and humility in your back pocket.

And hey, remember, leadership isn't just about the destination; it's about the journey. So buckle up, enjoy the ride, and leave a trail of greatness in your wake. After all, "The only way to do great work is to love what you do."—Steve Jobs

12

THE ART OF BUILDING SOCIAL CAPITAL—NETWORKING YOUR WAY TO SUCCESS

Social capital—it's more than just a buzzword. Think of it as the web of relationships, trust, and goodwill that connects individuals within a community or network. It's the intangible resource that emerges from meaningful interactions, mutual support, and shared values. In simple terms, social capital is who you know, what those connections are worth, and how they help you and others succeed.

If life were a grand banquet, social capital wouldn't just be the feast—it would be the invitation, the conversation, and the camaraderie that makes the event unforgettable. Often overlooked but quietly powerful, it's the secret ingredient behind countless personal and professional successes.

So how does one cultivate this valuable currency? Fear not—I shall be your guide through the labyrinthine world of networking.

Why, you may ask, is social capital so vital for a sales professional? Picture this: you're a salesperson armed with the finest product or service in town, but without a network of connections, you're a knight without a horse. In the competitive arena of sales, relationships reign supreme. It's not just about what you know, but who you know and, more importantly, who knows you. But let's not confine the significance of social capital solely to the realm of sales. In every facet of life, be it professional or personal, your network is your net worth. Whether you're vying for a promotion, seeking mentorship, or simply looking for a reliable plumber, having a robust social capital can make all the difference.

Now, onto the nitty-gritty of building this elusive yet invaluable asset. Networking isn't about collecting business cards like Pokémon cards or bombarding unsuspecting souls with elevator pitches. No, it's about forging genuine connections, akin to cultivating a flourishing garden.

Firstly, let's debunk the myth that networking is reserved for schmoozers and extroverts. Even the most introverted of souls can master the art of networking by focusing on quality over quantity. Remember, it's not the size of your Rolodex that matters, but the depth of your relationships. One golden rule of networking is to give before you receive. Be a beacon of generosity in a sea of self-interest. Offer your assistance, share your knowledge, and be genuinely interested in others' success. As the old adage goes, "You can get everything in life you want if you will just help enough other people get what they want."

Furthermore, don't underestimate the power of serendipity. Some of the most fortuitous encounters happen when you least expect them. So, keep an open mind and be ready to seize opportunities, even if they come disguised as awkward office mixers or dreaded networking events.

Now, let me regale you with a tale that perfectly encapsulates the magic of social capital. Once upon a time, in the bustling streets of New York City, a struggling artist named Andy Warhol found himself at the epicenter of the 1960s art scene. His meteoric rise to fame wasn't solely due to his artistic prowess but rather his knack for building social capital. By surrounding himself with influencers, socialites, and fellow artists, Warhol transformed his circle of acquaintances into a powerhouse network that propelled him to stardom.

So here are some effective techniques for building social capital and mastering the art of networking:

Be Genuine

Authenticity is key. Approach networking with a genuine interest in others, rather than solely focusing on what you can gain. People can sense sincerity, and it forms the foundation of lasting relationships.

Alright, imagine you're at a networking event. You've got your name tag on, a firm handshake ready, and a smile that says, "I'm genuinely interested in what you have to say ... but also, I could really use some snacks right about now."

Networking isn't just about swapping business cards. It's about forming connections that go beyond the surface level. So, instead of mentally rehearsing your elevator pitch for the umpteenth time, try listening more than talking. Ask questions, show curiosity, and genuinely engage with the person in front of you.

For example, if you find out someone is passionate about underwater basket weaving (yes, it's a thing!), don't just nod and smile while secretly wondering if they've lost their marbles. Dive into it (pun totally intended) with genuine interest. Who knows, you might learn a thing or two about the art of weaving while submerged. And remember, authenticity isn't just about what you say; it's also about how you say it. So, be yourself. Unless you can be Batman. Then always be Batman. But seriously, people can sense when you're being genuine.

In the end, networking isn't just about what you can gain; it's about building meaningful connections that can enrich both your personal and professional life. So, go forth, be authentic, and who knows, you might just find your next business partner or lifelong friend ... or at the very least, someone who shares your love for obscure hobbies and terrible puns. Mastering authenticity in networking is a bit like mastering any skill—it takes practice, self-awareness, and a willingness to step out of your comfort zone. Here's a roadmap to help you navigate your journey toward becoming a networking ninja with genuine charm.

- **Know Yourself:** Understand your values, interests, and goals. When you know who you are and what you stand for, it's easier to authentically connect with others who share your values or can appreciate them.
- **Listen Actively:** Practice active listening. Instead of waiting for your turn to speak, genuinely listen to what the other person is saying. Ask follow-up questions to show that you're engaged and interested in what they have to say.
- **Be Vulnerable (But Not Too Vulnerable):** Share personal anecdotes or experiences when appropriate. Vulnerability can foster deeper connections, but remember to gauge the situation and share only what feels comfortable and relevant.

- **Find Common Ground:** Look for common interests, experiences, or goals that you share with others. Finding common ground helps establish rapport and makes the conversation more enjoyable for both parties.
- **Be Present:** Put away distractions and focus on the person you're interacting with. Be fully present in the moment, and show genuine interest in the conversation.
- **Practice Empathy:** Put yourself in the other person's shoes and try to understand their perspective. Show empathy by acknowledging their feelings and experiences without judgment.
- **Give Without Expecting Anything in Return:** Offer help, support, or resources to others without expecting immediate reciprocation. Genuine generosity goes a long way in building trust and rapport.
- **Follow Up:** After the initial interaction, follow up with a personalized message or gesture to maintain the connection. Show that you value the relationship and are interested in continuing the conversation.
- **Be Patient**: Authentic relationships take time to develop. Don't expect instant results or rush the process. Be patient and allow the connection to grow organically over time.
- **Reflect and Learn:** Take time to reflect on your networking experiences and learn from them. What worked well? What could you improve upon? Continuous self-reflection and learning will help you refine your authentic networking skills over time.

Remember, authenticity is not about being perfect; it's about being genuine and true to yourself. So, embrace your quirks, be kind to yourself, and keep practicing. Before you know it, you'll be a networking pro with a genuine charm that's hard to resist!

Listen Actively

Practice active listening. Pay close attention to what others are saying, ask insightful questions, and show genuine curiosity about their experiences and perspectives. This demonstrates respect and helps forge deeper connections.

Imagine you're a detective solving a mystery. When someone is speaking, be like Sherlock Holmes on a case—catch every clue, analyze every detail, and don't let anything slip past you. Not even the tiniest "aha!" moment.

Ask Insightful Questions

Channel your inner journalist. Pretend you're interviewing someone for the cover story of a magazine. Ask questions that delve deep into their experiences and perspectives. Think less "How's the weather?" and more "What's the most exciting adventure you've ever had, and did it involve a parachute?"

Show Genuine Curiosity

Pretend you're an alien. Imagine you've just crash-landed on Earth and you're trying to understand the strange customs and behaviors of humans. Approach every conversation with the wide-eyed wonder of an extraterrestrial visitor. "Tell me more about this thing you call 'pizza'..."

Demonstrate Respect

Think of yourself as a diplomat. Treat every opinion and viewpoint with the same level of respect you'd give to a delicate international negotiation. Remember, even if you don't agree, everyone's perspective deserves to be heard. Unless they're arguing that pineapple belongs on pizza. Then, well, maybe not.

Forge Deeper Connections

Picture yourself as a friendship blacksmith. Just like a blacksmith hammers away at metal to create something strong and durable, actively listening helps you forge bonds that can withstand the tests of time and distance. Plus, you get to wear a cool apron and wield a hammer. Metaphorically speaking, of course.

Remember, active listening isn't just about hearing words—it's about understanding, connecting, and empathizing with the person speaking. Mastering active listening takes time, practice, and a genuine desire to connect with others. Here's a step-by-step guide to help you hone your skills.

- **Be Present:** Focus on the present moment. Put away distractions like your phone or other devices, and give the speaker your full attention. Show that you're engaged through nonverbal cues like nodding and maintaining eye contact.
- **Listen Without Judgment:** Suspend judgement and preconceived notions. Approach each conversation with an open mind, and strive to understand the speaker's perspective, even if you disagree with it. Remember, you don't have to agree with someone to validate their feelings or experiences.

- **Practice Empathy:** Put yourself in the speaker's shoes and try to understand their emotions and experiences from their point of view. Reflect on what you've heard to show that you're listening and to confirm your understanding. For example, "It sounds like you're feeling frustrated because ..."
- **Ask Open-Ended Questions:** Encourage the speaker to elaborate by asking open-ended questions that invite deeper exploration. Avoid yes/no questions, and instead, ask questions like "Can you tell me more about ...?" or "How did that make you feel?"
- **Paraphrase and Summarize:** Paraphrase what the speaker has said in your own words to demonstrate that you're actively listening and to clarify any misunderstandings. Summarize key points periodically to ensure that you're on the same page.
- **Show Genuine Interest:** Show curiosity and genuine interest in the speaker's experiences and perspectives. Ask follow-up questions that delve deeper into their thoughts and feelings and listen attentively to their responses.
- **Practice Patience:** Active listening takes practice and patience. Be patient with yourself as you work on improving your skills, and be patient with others as they share their thoughts and feelings with you.
- **Seek Feedback:** Ask for feedback from friends, family members, or colleagues on your active listening skills. They can provide valuable insights and suggestions for areas of improvement.
- **Reflect and Learn:** Take time to reflect on your conversations and interactions. What went well? What could you improve upon? Learning from each experience will help you continue to grow as an active listener.

- **Be Persistent:** Mastery takes time, so don't get discouraged if you don't see immediate results. Keep practicing, stay committed to improving, and celebrate your progress along the way.

By incorporating these strategies into your daily interactions, you'll gradually become a master of active listening, forging deeper connections with those around you and enriching your relationships in the process.

Provide Value

Be generous with your time, knowledge, and resources. Offer assistance, share helpful information or resources and look for opportunities to help others succeed without expecting immediate returns. This generosity builds goodwill and strengthens relationships over time. Let's break it down.

Generosity of Time: Picture this: You're in a rush, but your friend needs help moving a couch that's as stubborn as a mule. Being generous with your time means putting on your superhero cape and swooping in to lend a hand, even if it means sacrificing your Netflix binge.

Generosity of Knowledge: Ever been the Sherlock Holmes of DIY projects? Sharing your expertise without holding back, whether it's how to fix a leaky faucet or decode the mysteries of calculus, is like being the Gandalf of guidance. Just remember, with great knowledge comes great responsibility... and probably a few follow-up questions!

Generosity of Resources: Ah, the age-old dilemma: your neighbor's lawnmower is on the fritz, and yours is lounging in the shed, sipping lemonade. Being generous with your resources means loaning out that trusty lawnmower because a well-kept lawn is a win-win for the whole neighborhood. Plus, who doesn't love being the hero of suburbia?

Offering Assistance: Whether it's helping a colleague debug their code or lending an ear during a tough day, offering assistance is like being the friendly neighborhood Spider-Man. You may not have Spidey senses, but you've got a knack for spotting when someone needs a hand, and that's pretty super.

Sharing Helpful Information or Resources: You know that feeling when you stumble upon a life-changing recipe for the perfect chocolate chip cookies? Sharing helpful information or resources is like passing on that golden recipe—except instead of cookies, it might be tips for acing a job interview or mastering the art of public speaking. Who knew generosity could be so deliciously rewarding?

Opportunities to Help Others Succeed: Ever played the role of matchmaker between a job seeker and a hiring manager? Being on the lookout for opportunities to help others succeed is like being the Cupid of careers. You might not have wings or a quiver of arrows, but you've got a knack for making professional love connections.

Building Goodwill and Strengthening Relationships: Think of building goodwill and strengthening relationships like planting a garden. You sow the seeds of generosity, nurture them with kindness, and watch as your relationships bloom like a glorious bouquet. Who knew spreading love and goodwill could be so green-thumb gratifying?

So, remember, in this grand adventure called life, sprinkle a little generosity wherever you go. You never know, your act of kindness today might just be the plot twist someone desperately needs in their story. Mastering the art of generosity is like honing any skill - it takes practice, patience, and a sprinkle of self-awareness. Here's a roadmap to becoming a generosity guru.

- **Start Small, Dream Big:** Begin by incorporating small acts of generosity into your daily routine. Hold the door open for someone, offer a genuine compliment, or share a helpful tip. As you build confidence, challenge yourself to dream bigger and tackle more significant acts of kindness.
- **Listen Up:** Pay attention to the needs and desires of those around you. Actively listen to others without interrupting or thinking about your response. Understanding what others need allows you to tailor your generosity to make a meaningful impact.
- **Embrace Empathy:** Put yourself in someone else's shoes and try to understand their perspective. Empathy is the secret sauce that makes generosity genuine and heartfelt. It's easier to be generous when you can genuinely connect with the experiences and emotions of others.
- **Practice Gratitude:** Cultivate a mindset of gratitude and appreciation for what you have. When you recognize the abundance in your life, it becomes natural to want to share

your blessings with others. Gratitude fuels generosity and creates a positive feedback loop of giving and receiving.

- **Step Out of Your Comfort Zone:** Don't be afraid to push the boundaries of your generosity. Challenge yourself to help in ways that may feel unfamiliar or uncomfortable. Stepping out of your comfort zone not only expands your capacity for generosity but also fosters personal growth and resilience.
- **Lead by Example:** Be a role model for generosity in your community and among your peers. Your actions speak louder than words, so let your generosity inspire others to pay it forward. Lead by example, and watch as your acts of kindness ripple outwards, creating a wave of positive change.
- **Reflect and Adjust:** Take time to reflect on your experiences with generosity. What worked well? What could you improve upon? Use these insights to refine your approach and adapt to the needs of those around you. Generosity is a journey of continuous learning and growth.

Remember, mastering generosity isn't about achieving perfection; it's about making a genuine effort to uplift and support others. So, embrace the journey, embrace the occasional stumble, and most importantly, embrace the joy that comes from making a positive difference in the lives of those around you.

Follow Up

After making initial connections, follow up promptly and consistently. Send a personalized email, connect on social media, or schedule a follow-up meeting or call to continue the conversation and solidify the relationship. Consistent follow-up demonstrates reliability and reinforces your commitment to the relationship. Try to keep the email light-hearted; I have shared below an example of an email that I would ideally write, just to give you an idea of what I am talking about.

Subject: Keeping the Momentum Going: Let's Keep the Ball Rolling!

Hi [Contact's Name],

I hope this email finds you in high spirits and with your inbox not overflowing too much! 😄

I wanted to circle back to our recent conversation and keep the dialogue flowing. Connecting with you was like finding the missing puzzle piece to my professional journey, and I'm excited about the possibilities ahead! As we discussed [mention topic or point of interest], I've been mulling over some ideas that I believe could be beneficial for both of us. But before I delve into those, I wanted to touch base and see how you've been since we last spoke. Did the weekend treat you well? Hopefully, it was filled with a good balance of relaxation and adventure!

In the meantime, I've taken the liberty of connecting with you on LinkedIn. Let's keep the virtual handshake going, shall we? Feel free to connect back whenever you get a chance.

Additionally, would you be open to scheduling a follow-up call this week? I think diving deeper into [mention specific topic or opportunity] warrants some real-time discussion.

Looking forward to catching up and continuing our journey together!

Warm regards,

[Your Name]

P.S. If you're a coffee enthusiast like me, maybe we can swap favorite blends during our next chat! ☕

Mastering the art of follow-up involves a combination of strategy, consistency, and genuine interest in building relationships. Here are some tips to help you become a follow-up pro.

- **Be Prompt:** Time is of the essence when it comes to follow-up. Try to reach out within 24-48 hours after your initial interaction to keep the momentum going.
- **Personalization is Key:** Tailor your follow-up messages to each individual and reference specific points from your previous conversation. This shows that you were attentive and genuinely interested in what was discussed.
- **Mix Up Your Methods:** Don't rely solely on email for follow-up. Utilize a variety of communication channels such as phone calls, social media, or even handwritten notes to keep things fresh and engaging.
- **Stay Consistent:** Regular follow-up is essential for maintaining relationships. Set a schedule for follow-up activities and stick to it to demonstrate reliability and commitment.
- **Provide Value:** Offer something of value in your follow-up messages, whether it's relevant information, helpful resources, or simply a listening ear. This reinforces your commitment to the relationship and makes your interactions more meaningful.
- **Keep it Light and Engaging:** Injecting a bit of humor or personality into your follow-up messages can help to make

them more memorable and enjoyable for the recipient. Just be sure to keep it appropriate for the context and the relationship.

- **Practice Active Listening:** Pay close attention to what the other person is saying during your interactions, and use that information to guide your follow-up efforts. This shows that you respect their input and are genuinely interested in their perspective.
- **Seek Feedback:** Don't be afraid to ask for feedback on your follow-up approach. This can help you identify areas for improvement and refine your strategy over time.

By implementing these tips and staying committed to nurturing your connections, you'll soon become a master of the follow-up game!

Attend Networking Events

Actively participate in networking events, industry conferences, and professional gatherings. These provide excellent opportunities to meet new people, exchange ideas, and expand your network. Approach these events with an open mind and a willingness to engage with diverse individuals.

Embrace the Awkward Introductions: Ah, the classic awkward handshake or fumbled introduction! Instead of letting it throw you off, embrace it. Laugh it off and maybe even start a conversation about the perils of awkward first encounters. Remember, we've all been there.

Find Common Ground ... or Create It: Whether you're discussing the latest industry trends or debating the merits of pineapple on pizza (a divisive topic indeed), finding common ground is key. If there isn't any, well, that's where your creativity kicks in. Maybe you both have a love for obscure '90s sitcoms or share a passion for miniature bonsai gardening. The possibilities are endless!

Avoid the Dreaded Monologue: Nothing kills a conversation faster than someone monopolizing it with a never-ending monologue about their achievements or opinions. Remember, networking is a two-way street. Ask questions, listen actively, and resist the urge to turn every interaction into a one-person show. Unless, of course, you're a stand-up comedian. Then, by all means, bring on the jokes!

Follow Up Without Stalking: So, you've made some promising connections at the event, now what? Well, resist the urge to come on too strong. A friendly follow-up email or LinkedIn message is great, but bombarding them with daily cat memes might be a tad excessive. Remember, there's a fine line between persistence and stalking. Let's aim for the former.

Dress to Impress ... but Comfort Counts: Sure, dressing to impress is important, but let's not sacrifice comfort on the altar of fashion. After all, hobbling around in pinching shoes or constantly readjusting an overly tight tie won't exactly help you exude confidence. Plus, who wants to spend the entire event counting down the minutes until they can ditch the discomfort and slip into some cozy pajamas?

Exit Gracefully: Eventually, the event will come to an end, and you'll need to make your exit. Avoid the classic Irish goodbye (vanishing into thin air without saying a word) or the awkward lingering by the door. Instead, bid your farewells with grace, exchange contact information with those you connected with, and make a mental note to follow up later. And hey, if all else fails, you can always employ the classic "emergency phone call" trick to make a swift exit. Just make sure your ringtone isn't set to "Despacito" at full blast.

Remember, networking events are as much about building meaningful connections as they are about enjoying yourself. So, go forth, mingle, and don't forget to bring your sense of humor along for the ride! Mastering the art of networking events takes time, practice, and a willingness to step out of your comfort zone. Here are some tips to help you become a networking pro.

- **Set Clear Goals:** Before attending an event, determine what you want to achieve. Are you looking to make new connections, learn about industry trends, or find potential collaborators? Having clear goals will help you focus your efforts and make the most of your time.
- **Prepare Elevator Pitches:** Craft concise and engaging elevator pitches that highlight who you are, what you do, and what you're passionate about. Practice delivering them with confidence so you can make a memorable impression on others.
- **Listen Actively:** Networking isn't just about talking; it's also about listening. Ask open-ended questions, show genuine interest in others, and listen attentively to what they have to say. This not only helps you build rapport but also allows you to uncover common interests and opportunities for collaboration.

- **Follow Up:** After the event, follow up with the people you met to keep the conversation going. Send personalized emails or LinkedIn messages thanking them for their time and expressing your interest in staying in touch. Remember to reference specific points from your conversation to jog their memory.
- **Seek Opportunities to Help Others:** Networking is a two-way street, so look for ways to offer assistance to others without expecting anything in return. Whether it's sharing relevant resources, making introductions, or offering advice, being generous with your time and expertise can help you build strong relationships and goodwill within your network.
- **Practice Consistently:** Like any skill, networking improves with practice. Make an effort to attend networking events regularly, both in-person and online. The more you put yourself out there and engage with others, the more confident and effective you'll become at networking.
- **Reflect and Iterate:** After each networking event, take some time to reflect on what went well and what you could improve upon. Use this feedback to refine your approach for future events and continue honing your networking skills over time.

By incorporating these strategies into your networking efforts and staying open to new experiences, you'll be well on your way to mastering the art of networking events. Remember, it's not just about collecting business cards—it's about building meaningful connections and fostering mutually beneficial relationships.

Utilize Online Platforms

Leverage social media platforms like LinkedIn, Twitter, and industry-specific forums to connect with professionals in your field. Engage in relevant conversations, share valuable content, and reach out to individuals who align with your interests or goals. Online networking can complement traditional networking efforts and extend your reach.

So, imagine you're on LinkedIn, the virtual water cooler of professionals. Instead of just lurking in the shadows like a job-hunting ninja, jump into the conversation! Share articles, comment on posts, and connect with folks who make you go, "Hey, they seem cool." But remember, don't be that person who sends out more connection requests than a desperate politician during election season. Quality over quantity, my friend.

Now, onto Twitter, the land of 280-character wisdom and occasional cat memes. Use hashtags like #IndustryInsights or #NetworkingNinjas to find your tribe. Engage with influencers and thought leaders in your field. Just be careful not to get lost in a Twitter thread spiral. You might emerge hours later, bleary-eyed, muttering about the latest industry trends and wondering where your day went. And let's not forget about those industry-specific forums, you know, the digital hangouts where people gather to discuss everything from the latest tech gadgets to the best way to brew the perfect cup of coffee. Dive into these forums like you're searching for buried treasure. Share your expertise, ask questions, and forge connections with fellow aficionados. Who knows, you might even stumble upon your future business partner while debating the merits of espresso versus drip coffee.

In essence, online networking is like throwing a virtual cocktail party. You want to be the charming conversationalist who leaves a lasting impression, not the awkward wallflower lurking in the corner. So, polish up your LinkedIn profile, craft some witty tweets, and dive headfirst into the digital networking pool. After all, you never know who you might meet or what opportunities await in the vast expanse of the Internet. Mastering online networking is like mastering any skill—it takes practice, patience, and a sprinkle of strategic finesse. Here's a step-by-step guide to help you become a networking ninja in the digital realm.

Define Your Goals: Before diving in, figure out what you want to achieve through online networking. Are you looking for job opportunities, seeking mentorship, or hoping to expand your professional circle? Clarifying your objectives will guide your actions and interactions.

Polish Your Profiles: Your LinkedIn, Twitter, and any other platform you use should showcase your expertise and personality. Use a professional yet engaging tone in your bio, highlight your skills and accomplishments, and upload a flattering profile picture (preferably one where you're not holding a fish or wearing a novelty hat).

Be Strategic in Connecting: Don't just connect with anyone and everyone. Be selective and focus on quality connections—people who share your interests, work in your industry, or hold positions you aspire to. Personalize your connection requests with a friendly message to increase your chances of acceptance.

- **Engage Authentically:** Participate in conversations that genuinely interest you. Share valuable insights, ask thoughtful questions, and offer support to others in your network. Remember, authenticity is key—don't try to be someone you're not just to impress others.
- **Share Valuable Content:** Whether it's industry news, thought-provoking articles, or your own content, sharing valuable information establishes you as a knowledgeable professional. Aim for a good balance of original content and curated material to keep your audience engaged.
- **Join Groups and Communities:** Explore LinkedIn groups, Twitter chats, and online forums relevant to your field. Engage in discussions, share your expertise, and connect with like-minded individuals. These communities can be goldmines for networking opportunities and industry insights.
- **Follow Up and Nurture Relationships:** Networking doesn't end after the initial connection. Nurture your relationships by staying in touch, congratulating others on their achievements, and offering assistance when needed. A genuine interest in others goes a long way in building lasting connections.
- **Track Your Progress:** Monitor your online networking efforts to see what's working and what isn't. Pay attention to metrics like profile views, engagement levels, and the quality of connections you're making. Adjust your strategy accordingly to optimize your results.
- **Stay Consistent:** Like any form of networking, consistency is key. Set aside time each week to engage with your online network, share content, and expand your connections. Rome wasn't built in a day, and neither is a robust online network.

- **Be Patient and Persistent:** Building meaningful connections takes time, so don't get discouraged if you don't see immediate results. Stay persistent, keep refining your approach, and trust that your efforts will pay off in the long run.

By following these steps and staying true to yourself, you'll soon become a master of online networking, forging valuable connections and opening doors to exciting opportunities in your professional journey.

Offer Help Before Asking for Favors

When seeking assistance or favors from your network, always offer help first. Build rapport and establish goodwill by providing value and support to others before making requests. This reciprocity fosters a mutually beneficial relationship built on trust and collaboration.

So, picture this, you're at a networking event, mingling with a bunch of folks, and suddenly you need a favor. Now, instead of just swooping in like a seagull eyeing a sandwich, you decide to sprinkle a little magic first. You spot Karen, who's been talking about her recent website revamp struggles. You waltz over and drop a casual, "Hey Karen, heard you're knee-deep in website landmines. Need a hand? I'm practically a wizard with WordPress." Karen's eyes light up like you've just handed her a golden ticket. She gladly accepts your offer, and you spend the next hour untangling her web of HTML woes. Fast forward a week, and you find yourself in a pickle needing someone to proofread your latest project proposal. Instead of feeling like you're pulling teeth to get assistance, Karen jumps at the chance to return the favor.

See, by offering help first, you've turned what could've been a transactional relationship into a beautiful dance of mutual support and collaboration. Plus, you've gained a reputation as the helpful hero of the networking scene. It's a win-win, sprinkled with just the right amount of charm and goodwill. Mastering the art of offering help before asking for favors is like learning to ride a bike: it takes a bit of practice, a dash of finesse, and maybe a few scraped knees along the way. Here's how to become a pro at it.

- **Be Proactive:** Don't wait for favors to come knocking at your door. Keep your radar tuned for opportunities to lend a hand, whether it's offering advice, sharing resources, or providing assistance in tasks.
- **Listen Up:** Pay attention to the needs and challenges of those in your network. When you hear someone struggling with something you can help with, swoop in like a helpful hawk (or maybe a friendly pigeon) with your offer of assistance.
- **Be Genuine:** Authenticity is key. Don't offer help just for the sake of reciprocation. Let your willingness to assist come from a genuine desire to support others.
- **Build Relationships:** Take the time to nurture your relationships. Get to know people beyond just their professional needs. Genuine connections are more likely to lead to meaningful exchanges of help and support.
- **Follow Through:** When you offer help, follow through on your promises. Be reliable and dependable. This builds trust and strengthens your reputation as someone others can count on.

- **Humor Helps:** Injecting a bit of humor into your interactions can make offering help feel more natural and less transactional. It lightens the mood and makes people more receptive to your offers.
- **Practice Gratitude:** When someone does help you in return, express your gratitude sincerely. Acknowledge their assistance and let them know how much you appreciate it.
- **Keep It Balanced:** While offering help first is important, remember that relationships should be balanced over time. Don't be afraid to ask for help when you need it, but make sure you've built up enough goodwill by offering assistance in the past.

So, strap on your helmet, grab your metaphorical bike, and start pedaling toward mastering the art of offering help before asking for favors. With a bit of persistence and a sprinkle of humor, you'll be cruising through your network with ease in no time.

Join Professional Associations or Groups

Become actively involved in professional associations, industry groups, or community organizations related to your field. These platforms provide opportunities to network with like-minded individuals, stay updated on industry trends, and establish yourself as a credible expert in your field.

Imagine professional associations as the ultimate networking playgrounds for grown-ups, where instead of jungle gyms, you have industry experts swapping business cards like they're playing a high-stakes game of Pokémon. Now, why join these groups? Well, aside from the opportunity to collect business cards like they're rare trading cards, these associations are like treasure troves of industry knowledge. You get to hobnob with the best and brightest minds in your field, picking up insights like loose change on the sidewalk. Plus, let's not forget the power of camaraderie. It's like being in a secret club, except instead of decoding messages with decoder rings, you're decoding the latest industry trends over coffee and stale cookies at networking events. It's a bonding experience, really.

And hey, who doesn't want to establish themselves as a credible expert? Imagine you're at a conference, and someone mentions a hot topic in your industry. Instead of nodding along like you're trying to dislodge a stubborn tic, you confidently chime in with your expert opinion, leaving everyone in awe of your knowledge. That's the power of being actively involved in these groups. Oh, and let's not forget the perks. Some associations offer discounts on conferences, workshops, and even certification programs. It's like getting VIP access to the hottest events in town, except instead of velvet ropes, it's all about having the right membership card.

Now, for the examples. Let's say you're a budding graphic designer. Joining groups like the Graphic Artists Guild or AIGA can open doors to collaborations, mentorship opportunities, and maybe even a few design competitions to flex your creative muscles. Or perhaps you're in the world of finance. Associations like the CFA Institute or the Financial Planning Association can be your ticket to rubbing elbows with finance gurus, staying ahead of market trends, and maybe even landing that dream job at a top investment firm.

So, whether you're chasing business cards or just looking to level up your professional game, joining these associations and groups is a surefire way to make waves in your industry. And who knows, you might even have a bit of fun along the way. The step-by-step below will help you to master the art of joining and leveraging professional associations and groups.

- **Research and Choose Wisely:** Choose associations that align with your professional goals and interests. Look for ones that offer valuable resources, networking opportunities, and events relevant to your field.
- **Become an Active Member:** Be active by attending events, participating in discussions, and volunteering for committees or leadership roles. Show your enthusiasm and commitment to the group.
- **Network, Network, Network:** This is about building genuine connections. Strike up conversations, ask insightful questions, and listen attentively. You never know who might become your next mentor, collaborator, or client.
- **Stay Informed:** Keep your finger on the pulse of your industry by staying updated on the latest trends, news, and developments. Attend workshops, seminars, and conferences offered by your association to expand your knowledge and skills.
- **Share Your Expertise:** Don't be shy about showcasing your talents and insights. Offer to lead workshops, write articles for the association's newsletter or blog, or present at events. Establishing yourself as a thought leader will boost your credibility within the group.

- **Give Back:** Pay it forward by helping other members whenever you can. Offer advice, make introductions, or mentor newcomers to the association. Being generous with your time and expertise will earn you respect and gratitude from your peers.
- **Evaluate and Adjust:** Periodically assess your involvement in the association and adjust your strategy as needed. Are you getting the value you expected? Are there new opportunities you haven't explored yet? Stay flexible and open to new possibilities.
- **Have Fun:** Last but not least, enjoy yourself! Networking and professional development don't have to be dull and dreary. Approach each interaction with curiosity and a sense of adventure. Who knows what exciting opportunities may come your way?

By following these steps and staying proactive, you'll soon master the art of navigating professional associations and groups like a seasoned pro. So go forth, network like a champ, and watch your career soar to new heights!

Follow Up with a Personal Touch

After meeting someone new, send a personalized follow-up message or note to express gratitude for the conversation and reinforce your interest in maintaining the connection. Reference specific points from your conversation to demonstrate attentiveness and sincerity. I have shared below an example of an email That I would ideally write, just to give you an idea of what I am talking about.

Subject: Great Meeting You Today!

Hi [Name],

I hope this message finds you well! I just wanted to take a moment to express my gratitude for our conversation earlier today. It was truly a pleasure getting to know you and chatting about [specific topic discussed].

I particularly enjoyed our discussion about [insert specific topic or interest]. Your insights on [specific point mentioned by them] really resonated with me, and I found myself thinking about it even after our conversation ended. It's not often that I come across someone with such a refreshing perspective, so thank you for that! I also wanted to mention how much I appreciated your sense of humor. Your witty remarks kept the conversation lively and engaging. It's always a delight to meet someone who can seamlessly blend humor with meaningful conversation.

I'm genuinely looking forward to staying in touch and exploring more of [shared interest or potential future plans]. Feel free to reach out anytime, whether it's to continue our discussion or just to say hello.

Take care, [Name], and let's make sure our paths cross again soon!

Warm regards,

[Your Name]

Mastering the art of sending personalized follow-up messages with a personal touch requires a combination of attentiveness, sincerity, and effective communication skills. Here's a step-by-step guide to help you master it.

- **Be Attentive During Conversations:** Pay close attention to the details of your conversation, including the topics discussed, any shared interests, and notable points made by the other person. This attentiveness will allow you to reference specific details in your follow-up message.
- **Take Notes:** If possible, jot down key points or interesting tidbits during your conversation. These notes will serve as valuable reference material when crafting your follow-up message later on.
- **Express Genuine Gratitude:** Start your follow-up message by expressing gratitude for the conversation. Let the person know that you appreciated their time and enjoyed speaking with them.
- **Reference Specific Points:** Incorporate specific points or topics from your conversation into your message. This demonstrates that you were actively engaged and listening during the interaction. It also shows that you value the insights shared by the other person.
- **Inject Some Personality:** Don't be afraid to inject a bit of your personality into the message. Use humor or witty remarks where appropriate to keep the tone light and engaging. However, ensure that your humor is respectful and aligns with the other person's sensibilities. (Although a daunting task, practice and experience will get you there!)
- **Express Interest in Future Interaction:** Clearly communicate your interest in maintaining the connection and continuing

the conversation in the future. Invite the person to reach out if they have any further thoughts or if they'd like to connect again.

- **Proofread Before Sending:** Before hitting send, take a moment to review your message for any typos or grammatical errors. A well-crafted and polished message will leave a positive impression on the recipient.
- **Follow Through:** Once you've sent your follow-up message, make sure to follow through on any commitments or plans discussed during your conversation. Consistency and reliability are key to building and maintaining meaningful connections.
- **Practice, Practice, Practice:** Like any skill, mastering the art of personalized follow-up messages takes practice. The more you engage in conversations and send follow-up messages, the more natural it will become.

By following these steps and continuously honing your communication skills, you'll be well on your way to mastering the art of sending personalized follow-up messages with a personal touch.

Invest in Relationship Building

Building social capital is an ongoing process that requires time, effort, and patience. Invest in nurturing and maintaining relationships with your network by staying in touch, offering support, and celebrating their successes. The dividends of strong relationships are invaluable in both professional and personal endeavors. Now, imagine that you're not just a savvy investor in stocks and bonds, but you're also a connoisseur of social capital.

Yes, you heard that right! It's like having a portfolio, but instead of numbers, you've got names, faces, and stories. Let me break it down for you.

Stay in Touch: Think of it like watering a plant. You can't just dump a gallon once and expect it to flourish forever. No, sir! You gotta sprinkle those texts, calls, and coffee dates regularly. Remember, a neglected relationship is like a neglected plant—wilted and sad. So, be the gardener of your social garden!

Offer Support: Be the friend who's there with a metaphorical umbrella when life rains down its problems. Whether it's lending an ear for a vent session or offering practical help, showing you've got their back strengthens bonds faster than superglue.

Example: Remember when Jerry's cat ran away, and I showed up with a poster-making kit and a determined spirit? That's the kind of support that seals friendships!

Celebrating Successes: Just like you'd pop open a bottle of champagne for a successful investment, pop open some smiles and high-fives for your friend's achievements. It's not just about being there in the lows; it's about being the loudest cheerleader in the highs!

Remember, folks, relationships are the ultimate long-term investment. They don't come with a prospectus, but the returns? Oh, they're priceless! So, go forth, build those bonds, and let your social portfolio flourish like never before! Mastering the art of relationship building is like becoming a ninja in the realm of social interactions.

- Be aware of some of the traits that are important in relationship building, such as active listening, being genuine, staying curious, learning from mistakes and so on. It's important that you give without expecting because you will anyway get multifold in return when you offer help, support or kindness without expecting anything in return. It's like planting seeds of goodwill – they may not sprout immediately, but when they do, you'll have a flourishing garden of relationships. These attributes may need a vulnerability on your part. Embrace it willingly. Don't be afraid to let your guard down and show your human side. Vulnerability fosters intimacy and trust, making your relationships more authentic and meaningful.

Remember, becoming a master in relationship building is a journey, not a destination. So, arm yourself with patience, empathy, and a sprinkle of humor, and watch your social skills soar. By incorporating these techniques into your networking approach, you'll be well-equipped to build and leverage social capital effectively, whether you're a seasoned sales professional or navigating the intricacies of your professional and personal life. So, dear reader, armed with these insights, go forth and cultivate your social capital like a seasoned gardener tending to a prized orchard. For in the garden of life, the fruits of networking are ripe for picking.

13

THE WINNING MINDSET—UNLEASHING YOUR INNER CHAMPION

In the bustling world of sales, where every conversation could be a make-or-break moment, there's a secret weapon that sets apart the champions from the rest: the winning attitude. But what exactly is this elusive quality, and why is it so vital for sales professionals, as well as for anyone navigating the twists and turns of professional and personal life?

Let's unravel this mystery, shall we?

Unveiling the Winning Attitude

Let's take a scenario. You're walking into a meeting, armed with your pitch and a confident smile. Your competition is fierce, and the odds seem stacked against you. But here's the thing: you're not just there to make a sale, you're there to win hearts and minds.

The winning attitude isn't just about scoring victories, it's about approaching every challenge with a mindset primed for success. It's about believing in yourself, staying resilient in the face of setbacks, and radiating positivity even when the odds seem daunting.

The Power of Positivity

Now, you might be thinking, "But isn't optimism just wishful thinking?" Well, not quite. Studies have shown that a positive mindset doesn't just make you feel good; it actually enhances your performance and boosts your resilience. Think of it as a self-fulfilling prophecy: if you believe you'll succeed, you're more likely to make it happen. Take the legendary salesman Zig Ziglar, for example. He once said, "Your attitude, not your aptitude, will determine your altitude." And boy, was he right! Ziglar's infectious positivity wasn't just a gimmick, it was the secret sauce behind his record-breaking sales figures.

Why Sales Pros Need It (and Everyone Else Too!)

Now, you might be wondering, "Sure, a winning attitude sounds great for salespeople, but why should the rest of us care?" Well, dear reader, the truth is that the principles of salesmanship apply to every facet of life. Whether you're closing deals or navigating office politics, a winning attitude can be your greatest asset. It's the difference between seeing obstacles as roadblocks or as opportunities for growth. It's what sets apart the leaders from the followers, the movers and shakers from the bystanders.

Developing Your Winning Mindset

But how does one cultivate this mystical quality, you ask? Fear not, for I come bearing wisdom (and a few tried-and-tested techniques).

Start with Self-Belief

Believe in yourself, even when others doubt you. Remember, if you don't believe in your own abilities, why should anyone else?

So, picture this, you're standing at the edge of a metaphorical cliff, ready to take a leap into the unknown. You've got your dreams, your ambitions, and a tiny voice in your head whispering, "You can do this!" That's self-belief, my friend. It's like having your own personal cheerleader, except that cheerleader is you.

Now, let's talk about doubts. They're like those annoying little pebbles that somehow find their way into your shoes when you're trying to walk a mile in someone else's. People might doubt your abilities, your ideas; heck, they might even doubt your choice in pizza toppings. But here's the thing: their doubts don't have to be your reality. Because when you believe in yourself, you're basically telling the universe, "Hey, I've got this!" It's like giving yourself a mental high-five and saying, "I trust you to figure it out, even if the odds are stacked against us." And yes, I get it. Sometimes believing in yourself feels about as easy as trying to juggle flaming torches while riding a unicycle. But that's where the magic happens. It's in those moments of uncertainty and self-doubt that you dig deep and find the courage to keep going.

Think about all the greats throughout history. From Thomas Edison, who believed he could illuminate the world with his lightbulb, to J.K. Rowling, who believed in the magic of her storytelling even when rejection letters were piling up faster than Hogwarts acceptance letters on Harry Potter's doorstep.

Mastering self-belief is like sculpting a masterpiece out of a block of marble—it takes time, patience, and a whole lot of chiseling away at self-doubt. Here are some handy tips to help you become the Michelangelo of self-belief.

- **Know Yourself:** First things first, you've got to know who you are and what you're capable of. Take a good look in the mirror and say, "Hey there, potential superstar!" Recognize your strengths, acknowledge your weaknesses, and embrace your quirks. After all, even Batman had his utility belt of gadgets and his fear of bats.
- **Set Realistic Goals:** Rome wasn't built in a day, and your journey to self-belief won't happen overnight either. Set yourself some realistic goals that you can actually achieve. Start small, like finally conquering that pile of laundry that's been lurking in the corner of your room for weeks. You'll be amazed at how good it feels to check things off your to-do list.
- **Challenge Negative Thoughts:** Your mind can be a bit like a toddler sometimes throwing a tantrum—it loves to latch onto negative thoughts and throw them around like confetti at a pity party. But you're the adult in this situation, so it's time to put those negative thoughts in timeout. Whenever you catch yourself thinking, "I can't do this," replace it with, "I can and I will, thank you very much!"
- **Surround Yourself with Positivity:** You know what they say, you're the average of the five people you spend the most time with. So, surround yourself with people who lift you up, cheer you on, and believe in your ability to conquer the world. And if you can't find those people in real life, don't worry—Taylor Swift's discography makes for a pretty great substitute.
- **Celebrate Your Victories:** Whether it's finally nailing that presentation at work or successfully making it through a yoga class without face-planting into your mat, celebrate your victories, no matter how small they may seem. Treat yourself

to a victory dance, a scoop of ice cream, or a well-deserved pat on the back. You deserve it!

- **Learn from Failure:** Let's face it, failure is about as much fun as getting a root canal, but it's also one of life's greatest teachers. Instead of letting failure knock the wind out of your sails, use it as an opportunity to learn, grow, and come back even stronger. Remember, even Thomas Edison had a few lightbulb mishaps before he finally got it right.
- **Practice Self-Compassion:** Be kind to yourself, my friend. You're only human, and humans make mistakes. Instead of beating yourself up over every little hiccup or setback, practice self-compassion. Treat yourself with the same kindness and understanding that you would offer to a friend in your shoes. After all, you're stuck with yourself 24/7, so you might as well make friends with the person in the mirror.

So there you have it, your guide to mastering self-belief. Remember, Rome wasn't built in a day, but with a little bit of determination and a whole lot of self-belief, you can build the empire of your dreams. Now go forth and conquer, you magnificent marble sculptor, you!

So, the next time someone tries to rain on your parade with their doubts and skepticism, just remember this: you've got your own umbrella of self-belief. And as long as you're standing tall under it, you can weather any storm that comes your way.

Visualize Success

Take a page from the playbook of athletes and visualize yourself achieving your goals. The mind is a powerful thing, and visualizing success can help make it a reality.

Buckle up because we're about to embark on a mental journey to success town! Picture this—I'm lounging on a beach chair, sipping a fancy drink with a tiny umbrella, and soaking up the glorious rays of accomplishment. Ah, feels good already, doesn't it? Now, let's get down to business. Visualizing success is like having your own personal highlight reel playing in your mind. You see yourself acing that presentation, sealing the deal with a firm handshake (or a COVID-friendly elbow bump; your call), and basking in the applause of your colleagues. It's like starring in your own blockbuster movie, except there's no need for CGI because you're the real deal.

But wait, there's more! Visualizing success isn't just about daydreaming—it's about manifesting your goals into reality. So, while you're envisioning yourself conquering the world, why not throw in a few power poses for good measure? Channel your inner Wonder Woman or Superman and strike a pose that screams, "I am unstoppable!." Imagine yourself giving an award-winning acceptance speech. Hey, success is all about rolling with the punches, right?

Mastering the visualization game islike becoming the Leonardo da Vinci of your own mind's eye. Here's a step-by-step guide to get you going.

- **Set Clear Goals:** Before you dive headfirst into your mental movie marathon, make sure you know what you're aiming for. Whether it's landing your dream job, acing that exam, or perfecting your golf swing, clarity is key. Write down your goals and keep them somewhere you'll see them often, like on your fridge or tattooed on your cat (okay, maybe not that last one).
- **Create Your Mental Movie:** Close your eyes and let your imagination run wild. Picture yourself achieving those goals with vivid detail. Hear the applause, feel the firm handshake, and bask in the sweet taste of success. And don't forget to throw in some special effects for good measure—maybe a dramatic slow-motion sequence or a triumphant soundtrack.
- **Engage All Your Senses:** Visualization isn't just about what you see—it's about what you feel, hear, smell, and taste too (in case your goal is to become a food critic, then by all means, taste away). Imagine the warmth of the spotlight on your face, the sound of cheers ringing in your ears, and the scent of victory lingering in the air.
- **Practice, Practice, Practice:** Like any skill worth mastering, visualization takes time and effort. Set aside a few minutes each day to immerse yourself in your mental movie theater. The more you practice, the clearer and more vivid your visions will become.
- **Stay Positive:** Your mind is a powerful tool, but it can also be a sneaky little trickster. Don't let negative thoughts creep in and sabotage your success party. Whenever doubt rears its ugly head, kick it to the curb.

- **Stay Flexible:** Life has a way of throwing curveballs when you least expect it. So, while it's important to visualize success, it's also crucial to stay adaptable. Be open to detours, roadblocks, and unexpected plot twists along the way. Who knows? They might just lead you to an even better ending than you ever imagined.

Remember, mastering the art of visualization is like sculpting a masterpiece—it takes patience, persistence, and a whole lot of imagination. So, grab your mental chisel and get carving!

So, visualize success, embrace it with all your might, and remember: the only thing standing between you and your goals is a little imagination and a whole lot of determination. Now go forth and conquer, my friend!

Embrace Failure

Yes, you read that right. Failure isn't the opposite of success, it's a stepping stone to it. Learn from your mistakes, dust yourself off, and come back stronger than ever.

Embracing failure is like adding a splash of spicy seasoning to the bland dish of life—it's what gives it flavor! Let me take you on a little journey through the land of mishaps and mistakes, with a pinch of wisdom.

Picture this, you're attempting to bake a cake for the first time. You follow the recipe to the letter, preheat the oven, and eagerly await the delicious results. But lo and behold, when you pull it out, it's as flat as a pancake! Now, you could throw a tantrum and swear off baking forever, OR you could laugh it off, figure out where you went wrong (maybe you mixed up baking powder with baking soda—honest mistake!), and give it another shot.

Failure isn't a neon sign pointing toward doom; it's more like a neon sign saying, "Hey, try this way instead!" Think of it as a GPS recalculating your route when you take a wrong turn. Sure, you might have to backtrack a bit, but you're still on the road to success. Let's not forget the classic example of Thomas Edison. When asked about his many failed attempts at inventing the lightbulb, he famously said, "I have not failed. I've just found 10,000 ways that won't work." That's the spirit! If he had thrown in the towel after the first few attempts, we'd all still be sitting in the dark. Mastering the art of embracing failure is like mastering any skill—it takes practice, patience, and a healthy dose of self-awareness. Here's a roadmap to help you navigate this journey with finesse.

- **Shift Your Perspective:** Start by reframing how you view failure. Instead of seeing it as a shameful defeat, see it as a valuable opportunity for growth and learning. Remember, even the most successful people have faced setbacks along the way.
- **Set Realistic Expectations:** Understand that failure is a natural part of the learning process. Don't expect to hit a home run every time you step up to bat. Give yourself permission to fail and view it as a chance to refine your skills.
- **Learn from Mistakes:** When you do encounter failure, take the time to analyze what went wrong. What factors contributed to the outcome? What can you do differently next time? Extract the lessons from each failure and use them to improve your approach.

- **Develop Resilience:** Resilience is like a muscle—it grows stronger with use. Cultivate resilience by bouncing back quickly from setbacks. Remind yourself of past successes and times when you've overcome challenges. Keep a positive attitude and don't let failure define you.
- **Take Calculated Risks:** Embracing failure doesn't mean throwing caution to the wind. It's about taking calculated risks and stepping out of your comfort zone. Assess the potential risks and rewards before diving in, but don't let fear of failure hold you back.
- **Practice Self-Compassion:** Be kind to yourself when you fail. Avoid self-criticism and negative self-talk. Instead, practice self-compassion and treat yourself with the same kindness and understanding you would offer to a friend in a similar situation.
- **Celebrate Progress:** Acknowledge and celebrate your progress, no matter how small. Every failure is a sign that you're pushing your boundaries and striving for something greater. Celebrate the courage it took to try, regardless of the outcome.

Remember, mastering the art of embracing failure is a lifelong journey. It's not about never failing but rather about how you respond to failure when it inevitably happens. So, strap on your seatbelt, embrace the bumpy ride, and enjoy the scenic route to success! So the next time you stumble and fall (figuratively, hopefully), remember that failure is not the end of the road, it's just a detour on the scenic route to success. So, dust yourself off, laugh at the absurdity of it all, and come back swinging. After all, the best stories often come from the most epic fails!

Surround Yourself with Positivity

They say you're the average of the five people you spend the most time with. So, surround yourself with people who uplift and inspire you.

First off, imagine your social circle as a metaphorical smoothie blender. You toss in your ingredients—your friends, family, colleagues, and maybe that guy you always chat with at the coffee shop. Blend them up, and voilà, you've got your personal smoothie of influences. Now, let's say you're spending most of your time with Debbie Downer, Negative Ned, and Drama Queen Darla. You're basically marinating in a concoction of complaints, pessimism, and unnecessary drama. It's like drinking a smoothie made of expired milk and old broccoli—it's not going to make you feel great, is it?

On the other hand , if you're surrounded by Sunshine Steve, Motivated Martha, and Creative Carl, well, now you're sipping on a smoothie bursting with positivity, ambition, and innovative ideas. It's like a refreshing blend of fresh fruit and a hint of optimism—a recipe for success and happiness. But let's be real, life isn't always a perfectly curated smoothie bar. Sometimes you're stuck with a few sour grapes or overripe bananas in your circle. That's okay! The key is to recognize the ingredients that uplift you and strive to spend more time with them. Maybe limit your exposure to the ones that leave a bitter taste in your mouth (metaphorically speaking, of course). Mastering the art of surrounding yourself with positivity is like mastering any skill—it takes practice, patience, and a sprinkle of self-awareness. Here's your roadmap to becoming a positivity connoisseur.

- **Reflect on Your Current Circle:** Take a moment to evaluate the people you spend the most time with. Are they mostly positive, uplifting individuals, or do they tend to bring negativity into your life? Be honest with yourself about how each person makes you feel.
- **Seek Out Positive Influences:** Actively seek out people who radiate positivity and enthusiasm. Attend networking events, join clubs or groups aligned with your interests, or simply strike up conversations with uplifting individuals you encounter in your day-to-day life.
- **Set Boundaries:** It's essential to set boundaries with negative influences. You don't have to completely cut ties (unless necessary), but limit the time you spend with individuals who drain your energy or bring you down. Politely excuse yourself from conversations that veer into negative territory.
- **Cultivate Gratitude:** Practice gratitude daily. Focus on the positive aspects of your life and the people who bring joy into it. Gratitude helps shift your mindset toward positivity and attracts more positive experiences and people into your life.
- **Be a Positive Influence:** Lead by example. Be the kind of person you want to surround yourself with. Offer encouragement, support, and positivity to others, and you'll naturally attract like-minded individuals into your circle.
- **Engage in Self-Care:** Take care of your own well-being. Engage in activities that nourish your mind, body, and soul, whether it's exercising, practicing mindfulness, pursuing hobbies, or spending time in nature. When you prioritize self-care, you'll be better equipped to attract and maintain positive relationships.

- **Evaluate and Adjust:** Periodically reassess your social circle and the impact it has on your life. Are there any relationships that no longer serve you positively? Are there areas where you could use more uplifting influences? Adjust accordingly to ensure your circle continues to support your growth and happiness.

Remember, mastering the art of surrounding yourself with positivity is an ongoing journey, not a destination. Stay committed to cultivating uplifting relationships and nurturing your own positivity, and you'll find yourself basking in the warm glow of good vibes in no time. Remember, it's not about ditching your friends or family entirely (that would be awkward at Thanksgiving), but rather being intentional about who you allow to influence your mindset and energy. Surround yourself with those who uplift and inspire you, and you'll find yourself blending into the best version of yourself. Cheers to that!

And that, my friend, brings us to the end of this book. Remember, life's too short to be stuck in a sitcom rerun of negativity. So, grab your remote control, switch channels, and tune in to the feel-good station of positivity!

As the great philosopher and eternal optimist, Oscar Wilde, once said, "We are all in the gutter, but some of us are looking at the stars.", let's keep our eyes on those twinkling stars, shall we? Until next time, stay positive, stay fabulous, and keep those good vibes flowing!

AFTERWORD

As we reach the end of this sales odyssey, I find myself reflecting on the journey we've taken together. From the dusty footprints of traditional salesmanship to the ever-evolving landscape of online communities and artificial intelligence, we've traversed through the realms of sales excellence, leadership, and personal growth. It's been a whirlwind adventure, filled with insights, challenges, and moments of inspiration.

Although we have gone through sales techniques and leadership principles, it's really a roadmap for personal and professional growth—a guidebook for those who dare to dream big and strive for greatness. Whether you're a seasoned sales veteran or a budding entrepreneur, whether you're leading a team or embarking on your own solo journey, the lessons within these pages will serve as invaluable tools on your path to success.

I sincerely hope that the wisdom imparted in these chapters will not only enhance your professional endeavors but also enrich your personal life. May you find inspiration in the stories shared, guidance in the strategies outlined, and empowerment in the mindset cultivated. And remember, the journey doesn't end here. It's merely the beginning of a new chapter in your own sales odyssey—one filled with infinite possibilities and boundless opportunities.

As we part ways, allow me to leave you with a quote by the legendary Zig Ziglar:

"You don't have to be great to start, but you have to start to be great." So go forth and start your journey to greatness today.

Wishing you all the success and fulfillment you deserve.

Anoop Murali